WITHDI
UTSA LIBRARIES

RENEWALS 458-4574

mfa *Publications, a division of the Museum of Fine Arts, BOSTON*

MFA HIGHLIGHTS american DECORATIVE ARTS AND SCULPTURE

Gerald W. R. Ward

Nonie Gadsden

Kelly H. L'Ecuyer

Melinda Talbot Nasardinov

Frontispiece: Cabinet, Herter Brothers,

about 1880 (p. 152)

MFA PUBLICATIONS *a division of*
the Museum of Fine Arts, Boston
465 Huntington Avenue
Boston, Massachusetts 02115
tel. 617 369 3438 fax 617 369 3459
www.mfa-publications.org

© 2006 by Museum of Fine Arts, Boston
ISBN 978-0-87846-698-6
Library of Congress Control Number:
2206932310

All rights reserved. No part of this
book may be reproduced in any form or
by any electronic or mechanical means,
including information storage and
retrieval systems, without written
permission from the publisher, except in
the case of brief quotations embodied in
critical articles and reviews.

All photographs are by the Photographic
Studios of the Museum of Fine Arts,
Boston, unless noted otherwise.

Edited by Emiko Usui
Copyedited by Denise Bergman
and Patty Bergin
Design and composition by Lisa Diercks
Produced by Terry McAweeney
Printed and bound at CS Graphics PTE LTD,
Singapore
Series design by Lucinda Hitchcock

Trade distribution:
Distributed Art Publishers/ D.A.P.
155 Sixth Avenue, 2nd floor
New York, New York 10013
Tel. 212 627 1999 Fax 212 627 9484

First edition
Printed in Singapore
This book was printed on acid-free paper.

 This publication is supported
in part by an award from the
National Endowment for the Arts.

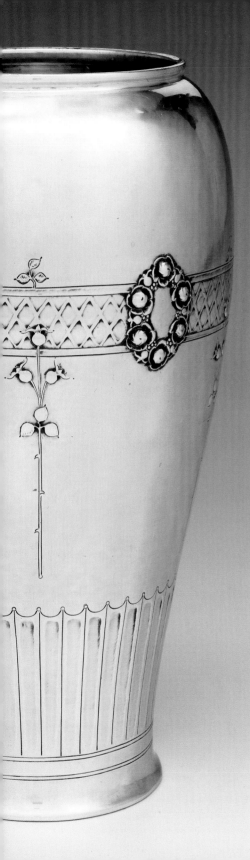

Contents

Director's Foreword

Art is for everyone, and it is in this spirit that the MFA Highlights series was conceived. The series introduces some of the greatest works of art in a manner that is both approachable and stimulating. Each volume focuses on an individual collection, allowing fascinating themes — both visual and textual — to emerge. We aim, over time, to represent every one of the Museum's major collections in the Highlights series, thus forming a library that will be a wonderful resource for the understanding and enjoyment of world art.

It is our goal to make the Museum's artworks accessible by every means possible. We hope that each volume of MFA Highlights will help you to know and understand our encyclopedic collections and to make your own discoveries among their riches.

Malcolm Rogers
Ann and Graham Gund Director
Museum of Fine Arts, Boston

Acknowledgments

We are especially grateful to Malcolm Rogers, Ann and Graham Gund Director, for his vision of creating a series of "highlights" books featuring the Museum's diverse collection. He, along with Katie Getchell, deputy director, curatorial, have given their enthusiastic support to this endeavor.

Like the works of art included in this book, this publication is the work of many hands. In particular, it has been made possible by MFA Publications, including Mark Polizzotti, director of intellectual property and publisher; Emiko Usui, senior editor; Sarah McGaughey, associate editor; Terry McAweeney, production manager; and Lisa Diercks, designer.

In the Department of Art of the Americas, we are especially indebted to Elliot Bostwick Davis, the John Moors Cabot Chair, for her enthusiastic support of the project and her close reading of the manuscript. Our paintings colleagues in the department, Erica Hirshler, Carol Troyen, Karen Quinn, Janet Comey, and Katy Mrachek, advised and reviewed our work as needed, while Patrick McMahon, Danielle Archibald Kachapis, and Toni Pullman offered assistance at every step. Volunteers Laura Conover and Pat Warner were also of invaluable help in assembling research materials for the entries.

In preparation for this book, each of the objects to be discussed and illustrated was examined and, in many instances, treated by members of the Museum's exceptional conservation staff. The efforts of Gordon Hanlon, Angela Meinecke, Daniel Hausdorf, Pamela Hatchfield, Susanne Gansicke, Mei-An Tsu, and Martha Shaw have made each object look its best.

Any project involving decorative arts and sculpture at the Museum is heavily reliant on the skills of our collections care staff, including Brett Angell, Eric Wolin, Mary Lister, Caleb Hammond, and James Cain. Julia McCarthy, manager of collections documentation, has been, as always, inordinately helpful in myriad ways.

The beautiful photographs of John Woolf, David Mathews, Mike Gould, and

Greg Heins present each object in this volume to its best advantage, and we are grateful to each of them for their enthusiastic support of this project. Christine Pollock, visual archives recorder, kept track of the many images needed for this project. Kerry Greaves, grants officer, foundation and government relations, was instrumental in obtaining funding for this book, and we are very grateful to the National Endowment for the Arts for the financial support that has provided us with this opportunity to present our collection to a wide popular audience.

Much of the material in this book is based on research conducted by prior curators of American decorative arts and sculpture at the Museum. Edwin J. Hipkiss, Kathryn C. Buhler, and Richard H. Randall, Jr., in particular, published extensively on American objects from the late 1920s to 1971. We are especially indebted to Jonathan L. Fairbanks, the Katharine Lane Weems Curator of American Decorative Arts and Sculpture Emeritus, who acquired many of the objects in this volume during his tenure from 1971 to 1999. It was Jonathan's vision not only to deepen and strengthen the collection in its traditional areas of early Boston and New England work, but to expand its parameters to embrace many different regions and time periods, thus turning a rather provincial collection into one of national significance. Other curators and staff members during the last few decades, including Wendy A. Cooper, Wendy Kaplan, Robert F. Trent, Edward S. Cooke, Jr., Jan Seidler Ramirez, Jeannine Falino, Jane Port, and Rebecca Reynolds, contributed to this effort. Many of their books, catalogues, and articles about the collection are included in the selected bibliography, but their unpublished materials contained in the department's object and artist files have also been an invaluable resource.

In addition, several scholars and friends took the time to read drafts and offer comments, including David Wood, Dean Lahikainen, Sarah Fayen, Mark Tabbert, Donald Fennimore, David L. Barquist, and Barbara McLean Ward.

Finally, we would like to acknowledge the donors, anonymous as well as those named within, who made possible the Museum's acquisition of the "highlights" published here. Without their generosity, there would be no highlights, nor, indeed, any collection. It has been our pleasure to present this introduction to their remarkable legacy of giving.

Introduction

Gerald W. R. Ward

The Katharine Lane Weems Senior Curator of Decorative Arts and Sculpture, Art of the Americas

In the 1870s, American decorative arts — American things in general — were a hot topic. During those years, collectors were beginning in earnest to scour attics and barns for antiques, as the centennial anniversary of United States independence fueled an interest in locating and preserving the quaint relics of the founding fathers and their fellow citizens of the early colonies. While collectors and antiquarians were thus looking backward at American decorative arts, hoping to retain some traces of an increasingly distant past, designers and manufacturers were actively trying to refine current taste through improvements to the decorative arts of the present and future. Some American firms, particularly silver manufacturers, even began to challenge what was perceived to be the long-standing supremacy of European goods. American silver objects sent by Tiffany & Co. to the 1878 world's fair in Paris, for example, received international acclaim and were held by some observers to surpass their European counterparts in quality of design and craftsmanship.

From its inception, the Museum of Fine Arts, Boston (which was founded that same decade), was part of this nascent interest in American objects. The Museum not only collected "old" American decorative arts as documents of history and nostalgic evocations of the past, but sought "new" objects as works of art worthy of emulation by contemporary industrial designers and of study by the general public, especially newcomers to this country.

Collecting American decorative arts and sculpture began at the MFA virtually as the institution's doors opened to the public at the museum's original Copley Square location on July 4, 1876. Classical-style sculptures by Thomas Crawford and cameos by John Crookshanks King were the first acquisitions in 1874 and 1876, followed by the gift on January 1, 1877, of a Tiffany and Company mixed-

fig. 1. **Pitcher, Tiffany and Company** (1837–present), New York, New York, 1875. (opposite) fig. 2. **Details of** *View of Boston Common* (embroidered picture), Hannah Otis (1732–1801), Boston, Massachusetts, about 1750.

metals pitcher (fig. 1), a then-contemporary work that had been made for and exhibited at the Philadelphia Centennial Exhibition in 1876. Later in 1877 the Museum added examples of current art pottery being produced in Hugh Robertson's Chelsea Keramic Art Works, as well as significant collections of Native American ceramics and other objects. Additional acquisitions of sculpture and decorative arts would follow in these early years as the MFA sought to acquire specimens that would enhance the institution's ability to further its goals of melding "Art, Industry, and Education," the three key components of the Museum's initial mission.

fig. 3. **Cyrus E. Dallin** (1861–1944), *Appeal to the Great Spirit*, designed in Arlington or Boston, Massachusetts, cast in Paris, 1909.

Over time, the Museum — now located on Huntington Avenue, where visitors have been greeted by Cyrus Dallin's sculptural tribute to Native Americans (fig. 3) for nearly a century — has developed one of the country's most important collections of American decorative arts and sculpture. About one hundred examples have been selected for inclusion in this *Highlights* book. Even a quick perusal of the contents of this volume reveals several recurrent themes that bear articulation as critical points of entry in any attempt to understand American objects. First, the high-style works of art illustrated here, from the seventeenth century forward, are best understood in the context of international artistic movements, such as Mannerism, the Baroque, the Rococo, Neoclassicism, the various revival styles of the nineteenth century, the modernist modes of the twentieth century, and the ongoing craft revival. (One often hears the viewpoint that modern decorative arts are "international," while those of the seventeenth and eighteenth century were not. Nothing could be further from the truth.) One key to examining American objects within an international framework is to assess the appearance of any given object in terms of the degree of its independence from, versus dependence on, foreign influences. An evaluation of the balance of innovation and tradition in objects of all kinds is the key, in most cases, to understanding what is American about American decorative arts, whether the focal point is design, materials, construction techniques, or other factors.

An active, thoughtful process of selection, rather than slavish, derivative copying, usually typifies the best American work. Thus, many students of early American furniture, for example, have argued that the development of a distinctive regional ornamental style—as may be found with the carved block-and-shell furniture of eighteenth-century Newport (fig. 4)—represents a form of American exceptionalism. Other scholars have found elements of American independence in the colonial period in a persistent, probably provincial, preference for certain forms, such as the high chest of drawers (p. 64) or the humble porringer (fig. 5), long after they have gone out of fashion in Europe. Whatever the case, an understanding of American work in an international context—an environment embracing what historians increasingly refer to as the Atlantic world and the Pacific world—is essential.

Equally significant to the understanding of any object—American or otherwise—is the recognition that each is part of a continuum within a series of objects. The work of the great twentieth-century sculptor Walker Hancock (p. 187), for example, is enhanced by knowing that he was a modern successor to a figurative sculpture tradition that began in this country with Thomas Crawford (p. 110) in the 1830s, who in turn traveled to Rome to learn from European mas-

fig. 4. **Bureau dressing table,**
Edmund Townsend (1736–1811),
Newport, Rhode Island, 1765–85.

ters and to study the antique at first-hand. Moreover, as George Kubler noted in his *Shape of Time* (1957), even "anonymous" objects of more humble origin can be located within a series that stretches backward and forward through time. Each represents a solution to a given problem in design, and while some are innovative "prime" objects, others are replications, or variations on the idea. One of the great advantages of studying and displaying American decorative arts within an encyclopedic art museum is the opportunity to compare and contrast American things not only with their immediate temporal counterparts, but within a much larger range of material from many cultures around the world that can be seen, in three dimensions and across time, under one roof.

Another major point is the importance of place—of what is usually called "regionalism"—in the understanding of American decorative arts. American objects, like American people, have always spoken with a regional accent, created by a complex combination of consumer preferences and craftsmen's skills. Isolating and understanding these regional preferences and characteristics has long been a focal point of scholarship; indeed, the goal of much research on American furniture, for example, has largely been to determine where something was made. These shaping circumstances of a locale can include nearly innumerable variables, such as the ethnic background of the residents (often affecting design and construction), the availability of native and imported materials, the economic well-being of the area, and its proximity to trade routes and style centers.

Although knowing *where* and *when* an object is made is essential to assessing that object, it is equally important to understand *how* it is made and how its maker (or makers) selected and manipulated the materials used in its creation. An informed appreciation of the challenges and opportunities each material and technique presents to a maker is essential to understanding the final form, utility, and, in the end, the quality of any given object. The malleability of silver, the plasticity of clay, the warmth and color of wood, and the almost-magical properties of glass are only a few of the attributes that skilled artists and craftsmen have explored and exploited to their best advantage over time.

Ultimately, it is the hands, mind, vision, and heart of the maker that determines the quality of each object discussed here. Because the trajectory of each individual artist's career follows a unique path and because we are covering here a span of centuries, it is difficult to derive generalizations that can be applied to the collective experience of American artisans and craftsmen. It is true, for example, that early American craftsmen were free from the restraints imposed by the formal guild structure characteristic of English and European trades, but they also were limited by the lack of rigorous training that the ancient system of teaching and controlling "the art and mystery" of a craft required. This may be one determining factor why immigrant craftsmen, especially those trained abroad and with significant technical skills, have played such an enormously important role throughout history in the creation of American objects. This is evident not only as one might expect in the seventeenth century, as in the work of Hull and Sanderson or the Mason, Messinger, and Edsall shops, all (of necessity) first-generation immigrants from England, but can be seen in the works of art discussed in nearly every chapter in this book. Outstanding works by Henry Hurst, John and Thomas Seymour, Anthony Quervelle, Ignatius Lutz, the Herter Brothers, Johannes Kirchmayer, Elie Nadelman, and many other immigrants from around the globe grace the pages of this volume. It may be trite to consider the United States as a "land of opportunity," but its burgeoning population and often prosperous economy have consistently provided artists and craftsmen with markets for their wares and perhaps stimulated them to find easier and alternative

fig. 5. **Silver porringer, Thomas Knox Emery** (1781–1815), **Boston, Massachusetts, about** 1805–15.

methods of producing objects in order to satisfy that demand. Many other factors, such as the abundant supply of natural materials offered by the Americas and the savvy entrepreneurial spirit of many artisans, are often cited in general works on American craftsmen, but it is not an easy task to discern the significance of such characteristics consistently across time, space, and various crafts.

Immigrant craftsmen are but one key component in the diffusion of style to the Americas from other countries and areas, whether it be England, France, Scandinavia, Germany, Holland, Africa, or elsewhere. Immigrant patrons, themselves with different sensibilities and levels of taste, were an equally significant factor in the transmission of styles from abroad. Pattern and design books and other printed materials played a role in determining the appearance of American objects as well. Imported objects also served as important elements in the transmission of style. These relationships are illustrated in this volume in a discussion of Boston rococo-style chairs (pp. 76–77), only one of many possible comparisons that can be drawn.

Many of these immigrant artisans made significant contributions in the Americas as specialists: as carvers, upholsterers, turners, chasers, engravers, or practitioners of another specialized craft requiring intensive training. The three colonial silver sugar boxes illustrated here are good early examples of the contributions of specialists at an early date (pp. 44–45). They also demonstrate the fact that decorative arts objects—at least until the Arts and Crafts era and the modern Studio Craft movement, when the importance of individuality was self-consciously celebrated—tend to be "the work of many hands," especially high-style objects produced in urban shops. Shop organization, kinship relationships, the hierarchy of a given craft structure, the intersections between various crafts, marketing strategies, and the transmission of technical and mechanical knowledge from one generation to the next are other key points of analysis in interpreting pre-industrial as well as industrial decorative arts.

Aesthetics, design, materials, techniques, and artist biographies are the traditional focal points of object interpretation, of course, but objects truly have multiple meanings: they can be analyzed from many vantage points and avenues of inquiry and they can tell us much about economics, technology, labor history, marketing, social life, religious practices, consumer behavior, manners, and nearly every aspect of human thought and behavior. The highlights selected here, for the most part, are objects that have risen to the top of a collectively shared system of subjective aesthetic value judgments, but their high visual quality does not detract from the light they can shed on many issues. While most were owned originally by wealthy members of society, their makers and marketers tended to be from the so-called working class or middle strata of society. As functional works of art, the furniture and other decorative arts in this volume were meant to be used, and a consideration of their symbolic, as well as their utilitarian, functions in domestic, ecclesiastical, and other arenas of social interaction can tell us a great deal about the attitudes and values of their owners and users.

The collection also contains many objects, seemingly more prosaic than those illustrated here, that are of great importance in the realm of American things, broadly conceived. A major contribution of Americans to the history of decorative arts has been the democratization of material goods through innovative types of mechanized production. Beginning in the early 1820s, for example, as-yet-unidentified American glassmakers familiar with the technique of blowing glass into molds (a method invented by the Romans) conceived of the concept of mechanically pressing glass into metal molds, thereby greatly reducing the amount of labor and time necessary to produce a finished object. This innovation revolutionized the social history of glass, bringing elegant glass tablewares (fig. 6)

fig. 6. Pair of pressed glass tulip-celery vases, Boston and Sandwich Glass Company (1826–1888), Sandwich, Massachusetts, 1845–65.

into the households of many Americans for the first time. Similarly, American manufacturers embraced the process of electroplating silver (initially developed in England) in the 1840s and later, transforming the use of silver objects in the home (p. 137), allowing many consumers to possess objects with the look of sterling silver but at a fraction of the cost. A large pewter and Britannia industry also produced a massive body of tin-alloy objects (fig. 7) that enriched the tables and daily lives of middle-class American consumers in the seventeenth, eighteenth, and early nineteenth centuries, when nearly everyone ate and drank from pewter. The finest pewter objects—even humble plates and basins—display graceful curves and sophisticated moldings derived from design books of the kind used by architects and cabinetmakers of the period.

What is equally significant about objects, however, is their affective power to evoke emotional and intellectual responses of all kinds. On an individual level, objects possess the ability to serve as tangible embodiments of memories, associations, and experiences of the owner and his or her family and friends. This symbolic and associative capability is largely independent of the object's significance as a work of art or its intrinsic value. Objects of all types become what sociologists call "icons of continuity," bridging gaps between generations. The importance of objects as three-dimensional embodiments of memories is made manifest by the many objects in this collection given by donors in honor or memory of family members, friends, or other associates.

In some instances—as with the Sons of Liberty bowl by Paul Revere (pp. 80–81)—a manifold number of factors combine to create an object of not only personal, but of national and international significance. Fashioned in 1768 to commemorate a courageous decision by the Massachusetts's House of Representatives, the Liberty Bowl was used regularly in secret and seditious acts of secular communion by the punch-drinking Sons of Liberty, who were leaders in the American resistance to "the insolent menaces of villains in power," namely the English monarchy and its administrative minions. The iconography of the bowl also includes references to John Wilkes, the Magna Carta, and other cornerstones of the Anglo-American love of liberty.

fig. 7. Early American pewter, including (from left to right) wine cup, Peter Young (active 1775–95), New York or Albany, New York, 1775–95; flagon, Samuel Danforth (1772–1827), Hartford, Connecticut, 1795–1816; teapot, Thomas Danforth Boardman (1784–1873), Hartford, Connecticut, about 1804–60.

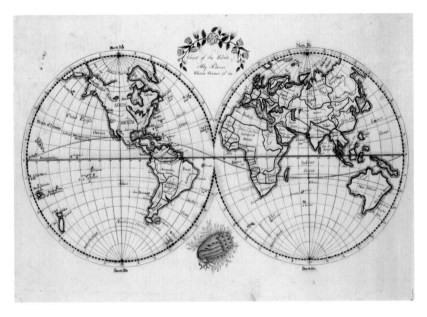

fig. 8. Abbey Perkins (active about 1811), *Map of the World*, Chelsea (now Norwich), Connecticut, 1811.

Passed down from generation to generation in the hands of the family of one of the original Sons of Liberty, the Liberty Bowl was acquired for the Museum in 1949, partly through the contributions of Boston schoolchildren, "as a symbol of our early struggle for freedom" and, presumably, a reminder of what was perceived to be the same sort of struggle then taking place in the Cold War.

The highlights here—selected for their high aesthetic quality, primarily using the parameters of traditional connoisseurship and arranged largely by style— are also thus historical documents of tremendous significance, illuminating the lives of the rich and famous as well as the existence of those who are often considered below the level of historical scrutiny. Art and history blend especially strongly in the decorative arts, which open many windows to "the world we have lost." The sheer diversity of American decorative arts and sculpture produced throughout the Americas (fig. 8), although only hinted at in this volume, is, not surprisingly, staggering. The consistently high visual quality of American work from generation to generation, however, may come as a surprise and, we hope, a delight to many readers.

Note to the Reader

During the last thirteen decades, the MFA has built an important collection of American decorative arts and sculpture, following different strategies. At this time, the collection includes more than twelve thousand objects, almost all of which have been gifts or have been purchased with funds donated specifically for that purpose. Martha (Codman) Karolik and her husband Maxim Karolik, who between 1939 and 1941 gave an outstanding collection of more than three hundred examples of eighteenth-century American arts as well as a significant body of three-dimensional folk art later on, are perhaps the most prominent benefactors associated with the collection, but it has been assembled in its entirety through the generosity of many individuals. Given the longstanding penchant for documentation among New Englanders, many objects in the collection are accompanied by a detailed history of ownership. Our collection, especially as represented by the "highlights" in this volume, is thus notable for its inclusion of many objects that, in a natural history museum context, would be considered "type-specimens": signed, dated, or otherwise documented examples that can be studied and used as benchmarks in assessing the quality, authenticity, and attribution of other objects.

"American decorative arts and sculpture" is a curious term and requires a brief explanation. As used here, it can be parsed as follows:

"American" embraces works of art made in North, Central, and South America—"the Americas"—from pre-history to the present, by both indigenous and immigrant peoples. However, since they will be treated in separate volumes, the outstanding works in the collection by the native peoples of the Americas are not included in this book.

"Decorative arts" refers not to paintings and prints—the most decorative of all art—but to three-dimensional, functional works of art, generally household goods such a furniture, silver, brass, glass, ceramics, basketry, jewelry, metalwork, and so forth. Some objects often considered "decorative arts" by other institutions, principally textiles, fashion arts, and musical instruments, are housed in several other MFA departments, who have or will publish their best American works in separate *MFA Highlights* books.

"Sculpture" includes here not only the traditional, largely figurative, three-dimensional works in marble, bronze, and other materials, but also coins and medals, largely designed by sculptors. American sculpture created after 1955 is not included here and will be part of a separate volume.

Most of the objects illustrated and discussed in this book are from North America, and a good percentage from New England. This is not surprising, inasmuch as most museums in the United States primarily have collected decorative arts produced in the region in which they are located. Although some of the earliest acquisitions of decorative arts by the Museum were coins from many locales in the western hemisphere, as well as objects from Mexico and South America, those acquisitions were not followed up in any systematic manner. By the late nineteenth century, the Museum's focus was fixed on "early American" objects, primarily from New England.

However, beginning with the creation of a separate Department of American Decorative Arts and Sculpture in 1971, the MFA sought to expand, in a strategic and systematic way, the temporal and geographical boundaries of the collection, recognizing that the Americas are a large territory rich in diverse works of art produced outside of the Anglo-American tradition. This effort was affirmed and enhanced by the Museum's creation of the current Department of the Art of the Americas in 1999. While the differences between the arts of North and South America are readily apparent, there are points of intersection and relationships that make an examination of the objects from all parts of the hemisphere a useful exercise. This approach has hardly been utilized to date in the study of decorative arts. As time goes on, however, the insights and understanding generated by the rigorous study of the interconnectedness of American art and material culture, broadly conceived, will only increase. We hope that this cross-section of the collection will provide the interested reader with an introduction to the extraordinary, and ongoing, artistic heritage of the Americas.

The Arts of New England in the Seventeenth and Early Eighteenth Centuries Gerald W. R. Ward

To some Americans, even today, the arrivals of the Pilgrims in Plymouth in 1620 and the Puritans in Boston in 1630 represent the beginnings of "America." This quaint, provincial, and outdated notion overlooks, of course, the existence of Native American peoples and the European colonization in Central and South America, the American Southwest, and Virginia that occurred far earlier. It similarly fails to take into account that extraordinary works of art were fashioned in the seventeenth century by, for example, skilled Dutch immigrant craftsmen in New York and the Hudson River Valley, English and German settlers in Philadelphia, English craftsmen in Charleston, South Carolina, and Spanish and Portuguese artisans in Mexico, Peru, and Brazil.

An impressive body of furniture and silver made before 1725 in New England has survived, however, and these objects have played an important, perhaps even disproportionate, role in shaping the nation's view of itself. The Museum of Fine Arts, Boston, has one of the largest and finest collections of such material, and although a few important early objects from New York, Philadelphia, and Quebec are among the holdings, this chapter focuses exclusively on furniture and silver from Boston, Salem, and rural areas of early New England. Produced by joiners, cabinetmakers, and silversmiths (or goldsmiths, as they were called interchangeably), these objects represent only a fraction of the domestic goods in use at the time. Pewterers, blacksmiths, at least one glassmaker, and earthenware potters were also active in early New England; their work, however, rarely survives. Stonecutting for gravestones, rich in Puritan iconography, was another highly skilled craft in this period (fig. 9), as were portraiture, practiced principally in Boston (fig. 10), and

fig. 9. Headstone for John Foster, attributed to the Charlestown Stonecutter, probably Charlestown, Massachusetts, 1681.

needlework. Already at this early date, the material culture of New England, and of the Americas as a whole, consisted of a rich blend of imported objects used alongside those made within a given region.

Early New England works of art, even those produced in the first years of settlement, are remarkably sophisticated, generally reflecting English and, ultimately, Continental versions of Renaissance, Mannerist, and, later, Baroque styles. Many of them, especially those made in Boston, were produced with the assistance of specialists — chasers, engravers, turners, carvers, and upholsterers — who operated within a complex and layered craft system.

Furniture making in Boston was established by immigrant craftsmen, including the London-trained joiners Ralph Mason and Henry Messinger, who arrived respectively in 1635 and by 1641. Thomas Edsall was a skilled turner when he emigrated from London in 1635. These men, who subsequently trained their sons and apprentices, established shops that dominated the woodworking crafts in Boston into the 1670s and later.

The Mason, Messinger, and Edsall shops produced high-quality objects in a London style of joinery, often making use of exotic imported tropical hardwoods. A second school of London-style woodworking developed along parallel lines in the New Haven Colony along the Connecticut coast. Elsewhere, from Essex County in the east to the hamlets of the Connecticut River Valley in the west, joiners produced oak and pine furniture in distinctive regional types that also can be traced to English prototypes from East Anglia, the West Country, or other regions of the mother country. Cupboards, chests, boxes, tables, and seating furniture were the principal forms made. Low-relief carving, painted decoration, applied turnings, and moldings embellished and enlivened these objects, which were generally low in stance, broad in proportions, and sturdy in construction. Their ornament was comprised of floral, architectural, and other motifs drawn from Renaissance and, in some cases, more exaggerated and exotic Mannerist modes.

By contrast, silversmithing in seventeenth-century America was a luxury craft confined almost exclusively to New York and Boston. In Boston, silversmithing began with the partnership of John Hull and Robert Sanderson Sr. in 1652 and grew to a trade with more than eighty silversmiths active at various times before 1730. Hull and Sanderson trained local craftsmen, including Jeremiah Dummer, the first native-born American silversmith, to produce silver for wealthy merchants and ministers throughout the region, as well as for the congregational and other New England churches. The churches used domestic forms — wine cups, beakers, two-handled cups, tankards, flagons, and bowls — when observing the sacraments of communion and baptism.

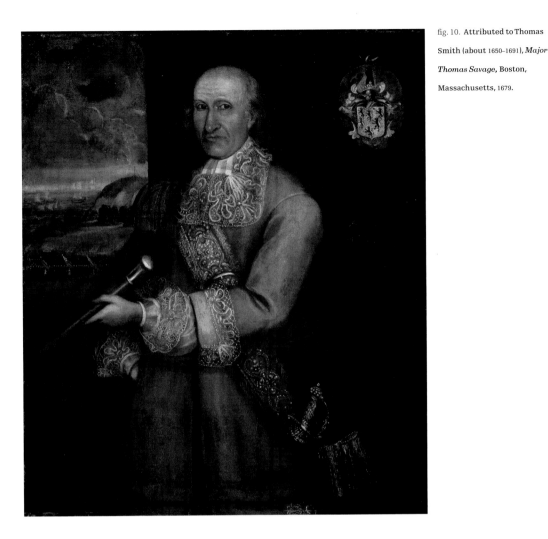

fig. 10. Attributed to Thomas Smith (about 1650–1691), *Major Thomas Savage*, Boston, Massachusetts, 1679.

During his long career from the 1680s until his death in 1722, John Coney produced the earliest American examples of many types of silver, including the first pots for tea and chocolate, in addition to such other ambitious forms as a punch bowl, an inkstand, sugar boxes, candlesticks, casters, monteiths, and plates. As with Boston furniture, the ornament on the finest Boston silver of this period can often be attributed to a skilled immigrant specialist, such as Edward Webb, Henry Hurst, or William Rouse.

At the end of the seventeenth century, a technological shift occurred in the making of case furniture from joinery (in which frame-and-panel carcasses were secured with mortise-and-tenon joints) to cabinetmaking (in which the maker created a carcass, often made of a local wood such as pine, using dovetailed joints, and glued thin slices of veneer to the exterior). Cabinetmaking allowed for more vertically oriented pieces in the new Baroque style, which often featured dazzling optical effects created by swirling burl veneers. Similar results were achieved in silver through the shimmering reflection of light on gadrooned surfaces and the contrast between smooth and adorned surfaces.

In the late seventeenth and early eighteenth centuries, Boston experienced an efflorescence in the arts as an influx of royal officials after the establishment of the commonwealth in 1692 attracted new generations of immigrant craftsmen to the emerging provincial city. Works of art made at that time—among them the Warland family chest-on-chest and the London-style silver made by Coney and others—are strikingly English in form and construction (see pp. 51 and 49). They represent in three-dimensional, tangible form the close cultural ties between Boston and London at the beginning of the eighteenth century that were also evident in architecture, literature, dress, religion, and nearly every aspect of social and material life. This strong Anglo-American tradition would remain the dominant theme in New England throughout the eighteenth century.

Chest of drawers

Attributed to the Ralph Mason (1599–1678/79) and Henry Messinger (died 1681) shops; with turnings attributed to the Thomas Edsall (1588–1676) shops

Boston, Massachusetts, 1640–70

Oak, cedrela, black walnut, cedar, ebony

Produced at a time when most case pieces were simple chests or chests with a drawer or two below, this object—perhaps the earliest example of Boston furniture in the Museum's collection—is a full-fledged chest of drawers, an innovative form rarely made in America before 1690. This unusual form makes use of exotic tropical hardwoods in its construction and decoration: a type of ebony was employed for the turned spindles in the upper case, and cedrela (*Cedrela odorata*), along with black walnut, was used for the façade and sides of both the upper and lower cases. The use of imported woods from far-away locales reflects the impact of the English joinery tradition on American work, as well as the participation of

Boston's craftsmen in an international world of trade and commerce as early as the mid-seventeenth century. The Museum's chest of drawers is among a small group of London-style Boston furniture attributed to the combined shop traditions of Ralph Mason, Henry Messinger, and Thomas Edsall.

H. 130.2 cm, w. 119.9 cm, d. 58.6 cm
(H. 51¼ in., w. 47³⁄₁₆ in., d. 23¹⁄₁₆ in.)
Bequest of Charles Hitchcock Tyler 32.219

Beaker or tunn

John Hull (1624–1683) and
Robert Sanderson Sr. (1608–1693)

Boston, Massachusetts, 1659

Silver

H. 9.8 cm, diam. rim 9.4 cm, wt. 193 gm
(H. 3⅞ in., diam. rim 3¹¹⁄₁₆ in., wt. 6 oz. 4 dwt. 2 gr.)
Anonymous gift
1999.90

Wine cup

John Hull (1624–1683) and
Robert Sanderson Sr. (1608–1693)

Boston, Massachusetts, 1660–1680

Silver

H. 20.3 cm, diam. rim 11.4 cm, wt. 404.2 gm
(H. 8 in., diam. rim 4½ in., wt. 12 oz. 19 dwt. 22 gr.)
Anonymous gift
1999.91

This beaker (or tunn, as it was sometimes called) and wine cup, each marked by the partners John Hull and Robert Sanderson, were two of the first silver objects acquired by the First Church of Boston (founded in 1630) and were owned continuously by the church until their acquisition by the MFA in 1999. Together, the vessels represent the beginnings of silversmithing in British North America.

The beaker and wine cup were the most common silver forms used by early New England churches in the sacrament of communion. Congregations generally acquired their silver through gifts or bequests. For example, John Winthrop, a founding member and prominent Puritan leader, presented to the First Church a large London-made cup of 1610/11 that he presumably brought with him from England. By the 1650s, however, parishioners could order silver made by Boston craftsmen. One of the church's first local acquisitions was a beaker made by John Hull before 1652 (when he formed his partnership with Sanderson). It is the only known object

bearing Hull's mark alone and is similar in style to the Museum's example. By 1680 the church had acquired seven objects made by Hull and Sanderson jointly.

The Museum's beaker is engraved simply "T / BC" for "The Boston Church" and "1659"; presumably it was acquired, either as a purchase or as a gift from an unknown donor, in that year. The wine cup, similarly engraved with the church's initials, in addition bears the inscription "The Gift of a Freinde T*C." It has been suggested that the initials are those of Thomas Clarke, a wealthy merchant and active member of the church. Clarke may have owned this cup originally, or it might have been purchased with funds generated by his bequest of £50 to the church.

Leather great chair

Salem, Massachusetts, 1665–80

Oak, maple; original upholstery foundation of linen
webbing, linen sackcloth, and grass; leather cover;
brass nails

In seventeenth-century New England, the upholsterer's craft was a luxury trade that, like silversmithing, was principally confined to Boston and, to a
lesser extent, Salem. Miraculously, this "great chair"
(a period term for armchair) retains both its original
Russia leather upholstery secured with brass tacks
and its original upholstery foundation of linen webbing, linen sackcloth, and stuffing of spike grass (*Dis-
tichlis spicata*) harvested from the tidal salt marshes
along the Atlantic and Gulf coasts. (Early photographs show the chair upholstered with a nineteenth-
century black oilcloth, which probably inadvertently
enabled the preservation of the original materials.)
The design of the chair calls for a large down-filled
squab, or cushion (a modern reproduction is shown
here), both to provide comfort for the sitter and to
visually fill the large void between the seat and the
high back.

In keeping with its status as a luxury product, the
chair was owned originally by Dr. Zerubbabel Endicott of Salem, Massachusetts, a well-known surgeon
and son of John Endicott, who served as deputy governor and governor of the Massachusetts Bay Colony
at various times in the 1640s, 1650s, and 1660s. It is
probably one of a set of two great chairs and six side
chairs listed in Zerubbabel's estate inventory.
Although the chair has been attributed to a Boston
shop for many years, recent research suggests that it
was probably made in Salem.

H. 96.5 cm, w. 60 cm, d. 41.6 cm (H. 38 in., w. 23⅝ in., d. 16⅜ in.)
Seth K. Sweetser Fund   1977.711

Chest of drawers with doors

New Haven, Connecticut, 1670–1700
Oak, walnut, cedar, pine

Among the types of London-style joinery practiced in seventeenth-century New England, one is associated with the Mason and Messinger shops of Boston (see p. 29), while another—seen here—is reflected in furniture made in the New Haven Colony by London-trained immigrant craftsmen, such as William Russell and William Gibbons. The inlaid checkerboard and sawtooth motifs, decorative spindles with unusual acorn caps, and frieze glyphs featured on this chest of drawers with doors are also seen on cupboards, chests, and other forms from this tradition. These New Haven objects also share an economical use of materials in their construction, perhaps reflecting the so-called wood famine mentality that permeated the thinking of London craftsmen, who were faced with a shortage of timber dating to Elizabethan times. Although lumber was plentiful in the American colonies, some immigrant craftsmen retained the frugal practice learned in their training.

H. 92.4 cm, w. 112.7 cm, d. 57.8 cm
(H. 36⅜ in., w. 44⅜ in., d. 22¾ in.)
Edwin E. Jack Fund   1980.274

Salver

Timothy Dwight (1664–1691/92)

Boston, Massachusetts, about 1690

Silver

Basically a large plate supported by a central foot, this salver (or server) is a great rarity in early American silver, not because of its form, but because of its maker and its decoration. Timothy Dwight, who apprenticed with John Hull and Robert Sanderson, was only thirty-eight years old when he died from "a sore and languishing sickness." This salver and an engraved tankard are the only objects bearing his mark known to survive.

What distinguishes the Dwight salver is its beautifully engraved border, with images of a camel, lion, elephant, and unicorn separated by scrolling leaves

and carnations. The identity of the artist responsible for this engraving remains unknown; it may have been Dwight or an as-yet-unidentified specialist. Its ultimate source is a type of naturalistic floral ornament that was used in Germany as early as 1650 and migrated to the New World through immigrant craftsmen and prints.

H. 8.1 cm, diam. base 9.4 cm, diam. dish 28.7 cm, wt. 587.9 gm (H. 3³⁄₁₆ in., diam. base 3¹¹⁄₁₆ in., diam. dish 11⁵⁄₁₆ in., wt. 18 oz. 18 dwt.)
Gift of Mr. and Mrs. Dudley Leavitt Pickman   31.227

Caudle cup

John Coney (1655/56–1722)

Boston, Massachusetts, about 1690

Silver

European floral imagery, enriched by the addition of cherubs, is seen on this caudle cup as chased (or hammered) decoration. The high quality of this ornament suggests that it was the work of a London-trained craftsman in John Coney's shop. The cup was made for John and Mary (Brattle) Mico, perhaps at the time of their marriage in 1689. Caudle, a warm ceremonial drink of sack or another type of wine mixed with eggs, bread, spices, and sugar, was considered suitable for such occasions as weddings and baptisms, during which the cup was passed from hand to hand by the handles.

The cup eventually descended to Oliver Wendell Holmes, the famed Boston physician and writer. In 1848, Holmes penned the poem "On Lending a Punch-Bowl" as a romantic tribute to his family's "ancient silver bowl," which he describes as the work of an "Antwerp smith," brought to Plymouth on the *Mayflower*. This charming but mistaken notion is understandable given the cup's superb workmanship and European-style imagery, and the fact that early American silver was not well understood at the time. After tracing the cup's history, Holmes concludes:

I love the memory of the past,—its pressed yet
      fragrant flowers,—
The moss that clothes its broken walls, —the ivory
      in its towers;—
Nay, this poor bawble it bequeathed,—my eyes
      grown moist and dim,
To think of all the vanished joys that danced around
      its brim.

Such nostalgic sentiments, expressed with greater
frequency as the nineteenth century progressed,
served to stimulate the collecting of "Americana" that
continues unabated today.

H. 14.3 cm, diam. base 13 cm, wt. 835.9 gm
(H. 5⅝ in., diam. base 5⅛ in., wt. 26 oz. 17 dwt. 12 gr.)
The Edward Jackson Holmes Collection.
Bequest of Mrs. Edward Jackson Holmes 65.388

Joined chest

Attributed to Thomas Dennis (1638–1706)

Ipswich, Massachusetts, 1670–1700

Oak, pine

H. 77.5 cm, w. 112.7 cm, d. 48.3 cm

(H. 30½ in., w. 44⅜ in., d. 19 in.)

Gift of J. Templeman Coolidge 29.1015

Joined chest with drawer

Springfield area, Massachusetts, 1699

Oak, pine, maple, black walnut

H. 81 cm, w. 136.2 cm, d. 46.7 cm

(H. 31⅞ in., w. 53⅝ in., d. 18⅜ in.)

Bequest of Charles Hitchcock Tyler 32.218

Many woodworking shops were active in seventeenth-century New England, and ordinarily the sources of their furniture design can be traced back to specific areas of England. Two examples are shown here: one from Ipswich in Essex County of eastern Massachusetts, and the other from Springfield in the Connecticut River Valley, about 120 miles to the west. The Ipswich chest is related to those associated with William Searle, who arrived in Essex County from Devonshire, England, in 1663, and with Thomas Dennis, also from southwestern England, who married Searle's widow and is the more likely maker of this example. The shallow relief carving covering almost every square inch of its façade is evocative of the

Devon style, as is its original painted decoration, much of which has survived though muted by time.

Bearing the carved initials PK and the date 1699, the Springfield example was probably made as a dower chest. It has been suggested that it was made for Prudence Kellogg of Hadley, Massachusetts, who married Deacon Abraham Merrill of West Hartford in that year, but that supposition has yet to be confirmed. It is one of a large body of some 175 surviving objects produced between about 1680 and 1730 in the Connecticut valley from Enfield, Connecticut, to Northfield, Massachusetts, and embellished with the so-called Hadley motif of a tulip and leaf on a stem. It is also part of a small subgroup enriched with applied spindles and chevron inlay formed by contrasting heartwood (dark-colored) and sapwood (light-colored) of black walnut (*Juglans nigra*). This type of decoration and other elements of the chest have been linked to the regional furniture of the North Country of England, brought to the valley by an immigrant craftsman from that region.

Cupboard

Northern Essex County, Massachusetts,
probably Ipswich or Newbury, 1685–90
Oak, maple, white pine

The cupboard—used for the storage of
textiles and other goods and for the
proud display of silver, glass, ceramics,
and other costly wares—was one of the
most expensive and prominent articles of
furniture in New England houses of the
seventeenth century. Few examples are
as richly ornamented as this large one,
which is embellished with nearly the full
vocabulary of seventeenth-century ornament: shallow relief carving, seen here in
foliate panels in the wide drawer front;
crisp turnings in maple; moldings
derived from architectural sources; and
painted decoration, here in the form of
black paint used in imitation of ebony.

Recent research has linked this cupboard to a woodworking shop located in
the area of Ipswich or Newbury in northern Essex County, Massachusetts, where
at least ten woodworking families are
known to have been active in the second
half of the seventeenth century. These
craftsmen produced a substantial body
of sophisticated furniture, including
chests of drawers, tables, and cupboards
that belie their rural, and seemingly rustic, origin.
This cupboard is a late example from that tradition,
notable for the high quality of its turned pillars and
applied half-columns.

Although the cupboard and other furniture from
this shop are products of the Anglo-American tradition, they also owe at least some of their inspiration
to Parisian furniture from the last half of the six-
teenth century, particularly the architectural case
pieces produced in the Second School of Fountain-
bleau (active 1540–1590). These Parisian designs

spread through the emigration of craftsmen and
printed materials to provincial France, England, and,
eventually, New England, where they found expression in the work of American joiners and turners in
the New World.

H. 149.2 cm, w. 123.2 cm, d. 49.2 cm
(H. 58¾ in., w. 48½ in., d. 19⅜ in.)
Gift of Maurice Geeraerts in memory of Mr. and Mrs. William
R. Robeson 51.53

Joined great chair

Essex County, Massachusetts, 1640–85

Oak

Like the leather great chair on page 32, this armchair was a symbol of hierarchy and authority in a seventeenth-century home. Framed with mortise-and-tenon joints like a chest of the period (see pp. 39–40), it is decorated with crisp, low-relief carving, including a back panel with a bold guilloche band, formed of interlaced circles with rosettes at their openings. The front legs and arms are not turned, but are square in section, sawn to shape and then refined with tools such as a drawknife, plane, or carver's gouge.

The chair is one of at least six related examples now known; two others were also recovered in Essex County. All derive their form and ornament from East Anglian furniture of the period. Like many seventeenth-century objects, it has suffered losses and alterations over time. After the Museum purchased the chair in 1937, it undertook a restoration treatment designed to return it to an approximation of its original appearance, using a closely related chair at the Danvers (Massachusetts) Historical Society as a prototype. A later seat was replaced with the current oak planks, and repairs were made to the lower parts of the legs and the stretchers.

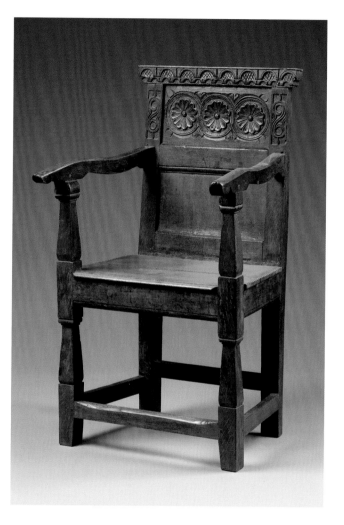

H. 103.5 cm, w. 57.8 cm, d. 42.2 cm
(H. 40¾ in., w. 22¾ in., d. 16⅝ in.)
Samuel Putnam Avery Fund 37.316

Tankard

Henry Hurst (1665–1717)

Boston, Massachusetts, about 1700

Silver

In seventeenth- and eighteenth-century America, the tankard was defined as "a large vessel with a cover, for strong drink," such as beer, ale, or hard cider. Silver examples varied greatly in size, from small tankards made for individual use to more capacious ones that held as many as four quarts to be passed from hand to hand around the table.

This tankard by Henry Hurst—one of only three known objects bearing his mark—is largely typical of Boston examples made in the late seventeenth and early eighteenth centuries, but the Swedish-style embossed fruit and foliage on its handle are extraordinary, perhaps even unique in American silver, because most American handle decoration is cast.

Hurst was born in Sweden, probably trained in Stockholm in the 1680s, and apparently worked as a journeyman in London in the 1690s. At the end of the century, Richard Conyers, a Boston goldsmith, contracted with Hurst to emigrate to America as his exclusive employee for two years, apparently recognizing Hurst's great skill in the specialty of chasing and embossing. Hurst and Conyers soon had a falling-out, and Hurst broke his contract. He then went to work in 1701 and 1702 for Edward Winslow. He may have been responsible for the elaborately chased sugar boxes that were produced in Winslow's shop at that time (see pp. 44–45).

H. 17.8 cm, diam. base 13.2 cm, wt. 816.5 gm
(H. 7 in., diam. base 5³⁄₁₆ in., wt. 26 oz. 5 dwt.)
Gift of Mr. and Mrs. Dudley Leavitt Pickman   31.228

Sugar box

John Coney (1655/56–1722)

Boston, Massachusetts, about 1680–85

Silver

H. 12.2 cm, w. 15.2 cm, d. 19.8 cm, wt. 886.4 gm
(H. 4¹³/₁₆ in., w. 6 in., d. 7²⁵/₃₂ in., wt. 28 oz. 10 dwt.)
Gift of Mrs. Joseph Richmond Churchill   13.421

Sugar box

John Coney (1655/56–1722)

Boston, Massachusetts, about 1700

Silver

H. 14 cm, w. 16.7 cm, d. 20.3 cm, wt. 711.5 gm
(H. 5½ in., w. 6⁹/₁₆ in., d. 8 in., wt. 22 oz. 17 dwt. 12 gr.)
Bequest of Charles Hitchcock Tyler   32.370

Sugar box

Edward Winslow (1669–1753)

Boston, Massachusetts, about 1702

Silver

H. 14.6 cm, w. 17 cm, d. 21.6 cm, wt. 708.4 gm
(H. 5¾ in., w. 6¹¹/₁₆ in., d. 8½ in., wt. 22 oz. 15 dwt. 12 gr.)
The Philip Leffingwell Spalding Collection. Given in his
memory by Katherine Ames Spalding and Philip Spalding,
Oakes Ames Spalding, Hobart Ames Spalding   42.251

Sweetness and silver were luxuries purchased at a great price—in both human and economic terms—in the seventeenth and eighteenth centuries. Inhumane slave labor was used to extract silver ore from the mines at Potosí and elsewhere in South America and to grow and harvest sugar cane in the West Indies. Wealthy consumers then expended considerable sums to buy the imported sugar and to commission elaborate silver vessels, such as these three sugar boxes, to hold the precious substance on their tables.

Of the ten known surviving American sugar boxes, nine, including the three examples shown here, are by John Coney or Edward Winslow of Boston, while one anomalous example is marked by Daniel Greenough of New Hampshire. Fashioned in the form of Italian *cassoni* (chests) and richly ornamented, these boxes are among the finest examples of early American silver. The elaborate chasing on each box may be the work of a skilled immigrant specialist. Nathaniel Gay may have been responsible for the chasing on the early Coney box shown at the top of the opposite page, while Henry Hurst may have performed a similar role for the Winslow example below.

In the seventeenth century, sugar was thought to possess special powers: one writer in 1637 argued that it "nourishes the body, generates good blood, cherishes the spirit, makes people prolific, [and] strengthens children in the womb." The iconography of the boxes alludes to marriage, fecundity, and fertility, making them "colonial expressions of courtly love" perfectly suited to house a material thought to contain reproductive and amatory properties.

Standing salt

Jeremiah Dummer (1645–1718)
Boston, Massachusetts, 1690–1700
Silver

Only three American silver standing salts are known to survive, all from Boston, including this example by Jeremiah Dummer, the first native-born North American silversmith. The two others were made respectively by Edward Winslow and the partnership of John Allen and John Edwards. It is thought that Dummer, who apprenticed to John Hull, in turn may have trained Winslow, Allen, and Edwards, as well as John Coney and several other Boston silversmiths.

English in style, Dummer's standing salt—used to hold the table condiment that at the time was relatively rare and thus worthy of an elaborate receptacle—is a good example of the early Baroque style. It features a smooth spool-shaped body, with an applied midband at center that contrasts with bands of reeding at its top and bottom. Supported by a hexagonal foot, the body is topped by an upper section with a shallow circular receptacle designed to hold the salt, and with four scrolled upright projections that are meant to support a covering napkin, plate, or vessel.

One of the leading silversmiths of his era, Dummer was also an active church and civic figure. At his death, an obituary in the *Boston News-Letter* noted that he "had served his country faithfully in several Publick Stations, and obtained of all that knew him the Character of a Just Virtuous and Pious Man." Dummer's sons Jeremiah and William, who became lieutenant governor, went on to achieve great prominence in Massachusetts politics and public affairs.

H. 14 cm, w. base 11.9 cm, wt. 329.8 gm
(H. 5½ in., w. base 4¹¹⁄₁₆ in., wt. 10 oz. 12 dwt. 6 gr.)
Bequest of Charles Hitchcock Tyler 32.371

Pair of candlesticks

John Noyes (1674–1749)

Boston, Massachusetts, 1695–1700

Silver

Candlesticks are rare in seventeenth-century American silver; only an earlier pair made about 1685 by Jeremiah Dummer and this pair by John Noyes—a skilled craftsman who is thought to have apprenticed with Dummer—are known to survive. Noyes completed his training in 1695 or 1696 and fashioned these hollow columnar candlesticks shortly thereafter for Pierre Baudouin (anglicized to Bowdoin), a Huguenot who immigrated to Casco Bay in Maine in 1687 and then settled in Boston, where he died in 1706. They descended in the Bowdoin family until presented to the Museum in 1954. One of the candlesticks' eighteenth-century owners was James Bowdoin, for whom Bowdoin College in Maine is named.

The general form of these architectonic candlesticks was popular in English, French, and Dutch

silver, brass, pewter, and ceramics in the second half of the seventeenth century. Like the Dummer salt (see p. 46), the Noyes candlesticks are in keeping with the latest London styles; they exemplify the best in the early Baroque mode, as light reflects and recedes off the small convex moldings on the base, flange, and removable bobeche (candle socket) of each stick, giving life to the surface and achieving the light and dark contrasts that are such an important part of this aesthetic.

54.594: H. 23.5 cm, w. base 16.2 cm, wt. 622.1 gm
(H. 9¼ in., w. base 6⅜ in., wt. 20 oz.)
54.595: H. 23.5 cm, w. base 16.2 cm, wt. 628.3 gm
(H. 9¼ in., w. base 6⅜ in., wt. 20 oz. 4 dwt.)
Gift of Miss Clara Bowdoin Winthrop 54.594–595

Chocolate pot

John Coney (1655/56–1722)

Boston, Massachusetts, 1701

Silver

Boston diarist Samuel Sewall visited William Stoughton, lieutenant governor of the Massachusetts Bay Colony, one morning in October 1697. They had "breakfast together on Venison and Chockalatte," and Sewall observed that "Massachusetts and Mexico met at his Honour's Table." A few years later, Stoughton left twelve pounds in his will to his niece, Mrs. Sarah Byfield Tailer, with the stipulation that she acquire a piece of silver as a "particular remembrance" of him. Stoughton died in 1701, and Mrs. Tailer apparently commissioned John Coney to make this chocolate pot— the earliest American example known —in fulfillment of his bequest. Graceful in form, and stylish even by London standards of the

time, Coney's work is a fitting demonstration of the ability of the silversmith to create enduring, functional works of art that delight the eye while also serving to perpetuate the memory, in tangible form, of family members.

In colonial North America, silver chocolate pots were a rare, sophisticated form used for what was then a new and exotic beverage produced from cacao beans grown in Central and South America. Most surviving examples were made in Boston, although some were also produced in New York. At least eight Boston examples, including this one, have survived.

H. 20.5 cm, diam. base 9.2 cm, wt. 580.9 gm
(H. 8 1/16 in., diam. base 3 5/8 in., wt. 18 oz. 13 dwt. 12 gr.)
Gift of Edward Jackson Holmes   29.1091

Caster

John Coney (1655/56–1722)

Boston, Massachusetts, 1710–20

Silver

John Coney was New England's most important silversmith from the 1680s until his death in 1722. The Reverend Thomas Foxcroft observed in Coney's obituary that he was "*excellently talented* for the Employment assign'd Him, and took a particular Delight therein." This small masterpiece in the late Baroque, or Queen Anne, style was made in the last decade of his long and productive career and evokes the "particular Delight" Coney enjoyed as a silversmith of the highest order.

Used for "casting" (or shaking) dry mustard, pepper, or sugar onto food, this caster is engraved with the Charnock arms for John Charnock and his wife Hannah (Holyoke) Charnock of Boston. The hexagonal baluster form, easily grasped by the user, is a superb expression of the elegant simplicity of the period, as are the graceful, delicate piercings of the detachable cover. Like the Warland family chest-on-chest (page 51), Coney's caster is a demonstration of the uppermost level of taste among Boston's wealthy citizens of the early eighteenth century.

The Museum's caster was originally one of two owned by the Charnock family. They descended to later generations and were recorded as "2 silver pepper boxes" valued at $6 in the estate inventory of Polly Dane, a descendant, in 1840. By 1963, when the Museum acquired this caster, the location of its mate was not known. Twenty years later, however, the second example reappeared and was sold at auction in New York.

H. 15.9 cm, w. base 4.9 cm, wt. 172.6 gm
(H. 6¼ in., w. base 1¹⁵⁄₁₆ in., wt. 5 oz. 11 dwt.)
Marion E. Davis Fund   63.956

High chest of drawers

Massachusetts, probably Boston,
about 1700–1720
Maple, walnut veneer, burl maple veneer, pine

Unlike thick, wide, seventeenth-century joined furniture, this high chest features dovetailed-board construction and is vertical in orientation. It is supported and raised from the floor by its six elegantly turned legs and feet, which are connected and strengthened by stretchers that echo the shape of the lower case's skirt. The drawers are veneered with a maple burl surrounded by a double band of walnut veneer laid in a herringbone pattern. The swirling burl veneers give the piece an exciting, visually active appearance, in keeping with the interest in optical effects of the new Baroque style of the early eighteenth century.

High chests, usually produced en suite with a dressing table, were designed for the storage of clothing and textiles in bedchambers, and their flat tops—sometimes fitted with a series of "steps"—were suitable for the display of small and valuable objects. High-style examples were made in the urban centers of Boston, New York, and Philadelphia. The Museum's high chest has a number of characteristics associated with Massachusetts work, including the contiguous arrangement of the drawers in the lower case and the use of native New England woods.

H. 161 cm, w. 101.6 cm, d. 54.3 cm
(H. 63⅜ in., w. 40 in., d. 21⅜ in.)
Gift of Hollis French   40.607

Chest-on-chest

Boston, Massachusetts, 1715–25
American black walnut, burl walnut veneer,
eastern white pine

This chest-on-chest appears at first
glance to be an English-made object, given
its broad proportions, walnut veneers, fluted
and canted front corners, recessed inlaid shell
in the lowest drawer, and "slider" (a pull-out
shelf, fitted with brass pulls, housed in the
mid-section of the object and used for folding
textiles and clothing)—all features characteristic of English furniture in the early eighteenth century.

However, the woods used in the chest's construction are American black walnut (*Juglans
nigra*) and eastern white pine (*Pinus strobus*),
both native to North America and characteristic of furniture made in America. Moreover,
according to microanalysis, the pollen
trapped in the hardened mixture of fats and
dust that adhered to the crevices of the piece
comes from trees, plants, and grasses characteristic of coastal Massachusetts and
Rhode Island. The chest is also known to have
a history of ownership in the Warland family
of Cambridge, Massachusetts.

Once it was recognized as an American-
made object, its relationships to other
Boston pieces in an Anglo-American fashion
suddenly stood out: the inlaid compass-
work star, for example, is found on many
other Boston case pieces, while the slider
was also popular in Boston. This chest and a few
related objects are the furniture equivalent of the
stylish silver made in Boston by John Coney, Edward
Winslow, and others, all testimony to a flourishing
artistic community in the first quarter of the eighteenth century and to the importance of London-
trained craftsmen who immigrated to Boston.

H. 178.8 cm, w. 107.3 cm, d. 54.6 cm
(H. 70¾ in., w. 42¼ in., d. 21½ in.)
Gift of a Friend of the Department of American Decorative
Arts and Sculpture and Otis Norcross Fund   1986.240

Arts of the Colonial Americas: The Eighteenth Century

Nonie Gadsden

The eighteenth century was an era of dramatic growth, adaptation, and maturation for the thirteen British colonies in America. A population surge from roughly 250,000 in 1700 to 2,500,000 in 1770, along with an accompanying rise in wealth, contributed to a great clamor for goods that scholars have termed a "consumer revolution." Although colonists had easy access to the latest London fashions via imported objects, immigrant craftsmen, and published designs, they increasingly relied on local artisans, especially cabinetmakers and silversmiths, to customize their orders and offer products more quickly and at a lower cost. The most prosperous of them, such as the Greenwood-Lee family pictured at right, aspired to live as comfortably and stylishly as their genteel countrymen in England (fig. 11).

fig 11. John Greenwood (1727–1792), *The Greenwood-Lee Family*, Boston, Massachusetts, about 1747.

The chairs depicted in the Greenwood-Lee family portrait (see far right of image) are in the late Baroque, or Queen Anne style, one of two design modes that dominated the arts in Europe and its various colonies for much of the eighteenth century. The style features symmetrical forms with sensuous curves and clean outlines decorated with highly figured veneers, intricate inlays, expert engraving, and other flat embellishments that do not break surface planes. Luxurious but restrained, the late Baroque exudes sophisticated refinement.

In contrast, the flashy Rococo, or Chippendale style of the midcentury is characterized by asymmetry, playful motifs, dramatically pierced forms, and dynamic, three-dimensional ornament that leaps from the surface. The Rococo is lively, spontaneous, and unrestrained — the opposite of its predecessor.

Colonial craftsmen of the eighteenth century emulated the late Baroque and Rococo styles coming out of London. They used imported objects, the work of recently immigrated craftsmen, and, by midcentury, printed designs as inspiration, sometimes faithfully imitating the pattern, but at other times creating their own variations that resulted in distinct designs and construction idiosyncrasies. These new interpretations came from several sources, including the ethnic background of the region's craftsmen and consumers; the individual skills and connections of local specialists such as carvers, turners, and engravers; and consumer preferences for specific forms and types of objects. Regional traits can help identify where an object was made; for example, a seat rail tenoned through the rear post of a chair reveals a German construction practice adopted by nearly all Philadelphia chairmakers, while decorative details such as a raked rear claw on a ball-and-claw foot, a bombé (swelled base), or a shaped, blocked (alternating concave and convex) façade indicate a Boston or New England origin. Such regional differences signify that American craftsmen had begun to develop and express their own distinct, local identities, separate from those of other regions and Britain.

American interest in independence and self-sufficiency came to the forefront in the 1760s, when the British government increased taxes on imported goods. The taxes not only sparked the widespread resistance that inspired the Nonimportation Agreements and ultimately the Revolution, but also encouraged ambitious entrepreneurs to develop American manufacturing. Because the production of ceramics, glass, and textiles required large investments of capital, colonial manufacture had been impractical when imports were available for reasonable prices. However, when the new taxes and higher prices fueled American patriotism and opportunism, several short-lived ventures were born, including Bonnin and Morris's porcelain factory in Philadelphia and John Frederick Amelung's glass factory in Maryland. Despite these valiant attempts, capital-intense manufacturing did not flourish; small shops that produced furniture, silver, pewter, and utilitarian ceramics and textiles were responsible for the vast majority of objects made in Britain's American colonies.

The western hemisphere's colonies were not limited to those ruled by the British crown in North America. France had settlements in Canada, and Spain had colonized much of Central and South America, as well as part of North America's southwestern region. French and Spanish colonial craftsmen also followed the styles of their motherlands, creating regional interpretations that sometimes incorporated elements of indigenous design (fig. 12). In general, French and Spanish colonial works are robust and adventurous interpretations of the prevailing international late Baroque and Rococo styles.

The combination of cultures and ethnic traditions in America's colonies sometimes resulted in new, hybrid designs. As the late Baroque fell from favor and the Rococo was on the rise, many craftsmen mixed elements of the two

fig. 12. Tapestry cover, Peru, about 1600–1700 or later.

styles, experimenting with motifs of the newer fashion while retaining elements of the old. This retention of the familiar largely continued through the turbulent years of the Revolution. Although the Rococo style was replaced by Neoclassicism throughout Europe in the 1770s, it was not broadly adopted in America until the 1790s.

Desk and bookcase

Boston, Massachusetts, about 1715–20
Walnut, white pine, mahogany, ebony,
satinwood

The practice of adding a bookcase above a
slant-front desk developed in early eighteenth-century Britain as part of the newly
popular late Baroque style. Tall, substantial, and imposing, the combined desk and
bookcase was designed to look like a small
building. The lower desk serves as the
slightly wider, horizontally oriented, solid
foundation, while the upper section soars
to great heights, often featuring arched
doors, and capped by a pediment.

This elegant desk and bookcase is a
very early American example of the new
form and successfully incorporates many
characteristics of the late Baroque style.
The basic architectural form and strong
verticality of the Boston-made piece give it
a striking presence, while its narrow proportions, clean lines, and high-quality
woods lend an aura of sophistication and
refinement. The surface is enlivened by
swirling, highly figured veneers and an
array of inlaid designs in light and dark
woods, including bands in a checkerboard
pattern and five inlaid stars that create the
illusion of spinning. The interior of the
piece is lavishly fitted with stepped, undulating drawers, carved shells, and extensive pigeonhole compartments that held
important business and family documents.

H. 224.8 cm, w. 75.2 cm, d. 52.1 cm
(H. 88½ in., w. 29⅝ in., d. 20½ in.)
The M. and M. Karolik Collection of Eighteenth-
Century American Arts 39.176

Two-handled covered cup

Jacob Hurd (1702/03–1758)

Boston, Massachusetts, about 1740–50

Silver

This monumental two-handled covered cup is the epitome of American late Baroque silver. Jacob Hurd, Boston's premier silversmith of the mid-eighteenth century, combined complex moldings and wide, scrolled handles to create a balanced yet bold architectural composition. This cup was not only meant for drinking; it was meant to impress.

Majestic two-handled cups (also known as grace cups) were particularly popular in Boston, and Hurd alone is known to have made at least four surviving examples. Such cups were often given as a presentation gift or commemorative award and were regularly used as communal drinking vessels for large groups in taverns or private gatherings at home. The pair of handles allowed the vessel to be easily passed from one person to the next. Many two-handled cups bear an engraved inscription honoring a person or recording an event; this example bears the coat of arms of the Rowe family of Boston. John Rowe, the cup's first owner, was a merchant who also actively participated in Massachusetts politics and social life.

H. 34.3 cm, w. 30.5 cm, diam. base 14.4 cm, wt. 2367 gm
(H. 13½ in., w. 12 in., diam. base 5¹¹/₁₆ in., wt. 76 oz. 2 dwt.)
Helen and Alice Colburn Fund   36.415

Clothespress

Boston, Massachusetts, 1740–50
Mahogany, chestnut, eastern white pine

This clothespress once stored linens and other textiles in its eleven drawers, many of which are concealed behind the doors of the upper case. Despite its attractive design and high degree of utility, the form, which was introduced in England in the second quarter of the eighteenth century, did not gain a large following in Boston. This Boston-made example is therefore extremely rare. Several factors, including the continued popularity of other storage forms and the dramatic decrease in English-trained craftsmen in the city after the 1720s, may have contributed to its scarcity.

Although this clothespress is much taller than English versions, its design incorporates elements of the mature Georgian style, a heavy and robust version of the late Baroque common in Britain, but generally not seen in colonial American furniture. The Georgian elements of this piece include the thick doors of the upper case, the concealed clothes-folding board or "slider" at the waist, and the exaggerated curves of the Anglo-Dutch-style closed ogee pediment. The use of thin stock for the drawers and the overall drawer construction also followed current British practice, but the Boston-based craftsman of this piece used American woods, including chestnut and eastern white pine, for the drawers instead of oak, the typical English choice.

This clothespress was made for wealthy Boston merchant Gilbert DeBlois, probably around the time of his marriage to Ann Coffin in 1749. DeBlois was a Loyalist who fled to England during the Revolution, leaving his family and property behind. Ann DeBlois managed to retain the family possessions, or perhaps reacquire them after they were confiscated during the war. The clothespress remained in the family until it came to the Museum in 1987.

H. 230.1 cm, w. 114.3 cm, d. 56.5 cm
(H. 90¾ in., w. 45 in., d. 22¼ in.)
Gift of Friends of the Department of American Decorative Arts and Sculpture   1987.254

Side chair

Philadelphia, Pennsylvania, about 1740
Walnut, white pine

Unlike the rectilinear lines of the early Baroque style, the late Baroque embraced curves. This undulating Philadelphia side chair is sculptural in form with a sweeping arched crest rail and a bulbous rounded seat. Some scholars have argued that these curves came into fashion precisely because they were more expensive to make. Craftsmen on both sides of the Atlantic had learned how to mass-produce the straight, turned elements of the early style. Larger quantities made such chairs less expensive and therefore available to more people. In their effort to offer novel and more exclusive designs, craftsmen serving the wealthy began to create curved furniture that had to be carved by hand, thus slowing down production and greatly increasing costs.

The most boldly shaped American late Baroque chairs, such as this example, were made in Philadelphia. The city was becoming increasingly important — in both wealth and political power — just as this curved style was gaining popularity in the American colonies. Philadelphia's new prominence further attracted immigrant British craftsmen who brought the latest styles.

This chair's striking profile is enhanced by carving that emphasizes the piece's curves. Leafy tendrils flowing out of a carved shell stream down each leg, while a large, looser shell spreads over the crest rail between two dynamic volutes. A highly unusual flamelike motif creeps up the center toe of the trifid feet. Few chairs of this style surpass the opulence of this example, either in form or decoration.

H. 108.6 cm, w. 51.4 cm, d. 40.6 cm
(H. 42¾ in., w. 20¼ in., d. 16 in.)
The M. and M. Karolik Collection of Eighteenth-Century
American Arts   39.119

Missal stand (*atril*)

Moxos or Chiquitos missions, Paraguay, 1725–30
Silver, replaced wooden frame

When fifteenth-century Spanish explorers set out for the New World, they were searching for gold. Instead, they found an abundance of silver, which they started to mine and send back to Europe. To support this lucrative venture, Spain claimed the silver-rich territory (now comprising the southwestern United States, Mexico, Central America, and some parts of South America), set up a governing system, and erected churches with the plan of converting the native peoples.

Spanish Jesuits, members of a missionary sect of Catholicism founded in 1540, settled in Paraguay in 1607 to educate and convert the indigenous people. This early Baroque-style silver *atril*, or missal stand, was created out of local silver for a Jesuit church in Paraguay in the early eighteenth century. Composed of a wooden frame and five sheets of elaborately shaped silver, the stand held the clergy's liturgical books during Mass.

The iconography of the stand incorporates both Latin American and Spanish imagery. The Latin American symbols include local flora and fauna, such as the *vizcacha* (small plant-eating rodents with large ears) and passionflowers (a native symbol of resurrection appropriated by the Catholic Church to symbolize the Passion of Christ). Each figure flanking the central monogram combines the ancient pagan *hombre verde*, or green man—a symbol of life, nature, and fertility—with the square-necked costume of archangels. The monogram, "IHS" with a cross and three nails, is the seal of the Jesuit order.

H. 29.5 cm, w. 34.8 cm, d. 27 cm, wt. including wooden frame 2600 gm (H. 11⅝ in., w. 13¹¹⁄₁₆ in., d. 10⅝ in., wt. including wooden frame 83 oz. 11 dwt. 20 gr.)
Gift of Landon T. Clay   2001.843

High chest of drawers

Boston, Massachusetts, about 1730–40
Japanned butternut, maple, white pine

When European merchants started traveling to China and Japan in the late fifteenth century, they returned with exotic wares, including tea, silk, porcelain, and lacquerwork. The European aristocracy became enamored with the worldly mystique of these objects, and by the late seventeenth century demand soared, encouraging local craftsmen to imitate the imported wares. "Japanned" decoration, as it was known in the eighteenth century, is a greatly simplified imitation of Asian lacquerwork. When the technique and style reached Boston via England, it struck a responsive

chord, as evidenced by this outstanding high chest. In fact, the production of japanned furniture in colonial America was largely, if not exclusively, limited to Boston craftsmen.

Asian lacquerwork consists of many layers of clear, hard lacquer (sap from the Asian tree *Rhus vernicifera),* ornamented with raised and gilt figures and scenes. Without access to the same raw materials as their Asian counterparts, European and American craftsmen developed their own methods using local resources. Instead of multiple layers of lacquer, American japanners simply applied oil paint to tightly grained woods, such as the butternut of this high chest. The most common background on American japanned wares is solid black, which was created by adding lampblack to a resin. This high chest, however, has a simulated tortoiseshell background, a treatment predominantly seen in the 1730s and 1740s. To achieve this look, the japanner first applied a vermillion (red) layer of paint, then streaked the surface with lampblack in resin. Fanciful figures, animals, and flowers were then added, either painted on the surface in gold, or built up with gesso, gilded, and articulated with black ink lines. To complete the sumptuous effect, the entire surface of the piece was varnished to a glittering finish.

At least ten japanners worked in Boston before 1750. Several design characteristics link this example to work by William Randall and Robert Davis, among them the large animals and figures (see the dog on the third long drawer), oversized floral ornament (on the center of the second long drawer), long-necked birds resembling cranes (on the first and second long drawers and the skirt), and isolated, rather than integrated, groups of motifs.

H. 182.2 cm, w. 109 cm, d. 62.9 cm
(H. 71¾ in., w. 42⅞ in., d. 24¾ in.)
Bequest of Charles Hitchcock Tyler 32.227

Side chair

Needlework seat attributed to

Margaret Fayerweather Bromfield (1732–1761)

Boston, Massachusetts, about 1750–60

Walnut, white pine, maple, original needlework seat cover

fig. 13. John Greenwood (1727–1792), *Mrs. Henry Bromfield (Margaret Fayerweather)*, Boston, Massachusetts, about 1749.

This highly embellished chair is an elaborate version of a conventional Boston design. The standard shape, with a curved crest rail, solid, vase-shaped back splat, rounded seat, and cabriole front legs, is ornamented with carved fan-shaped shells on the knees and a bold shell flanked by delicate floral tendrils on the crest rail. This skillful decoration was possibly executed by Boston's premier eighteenth-century carver, John Welch.

This chair and five mates descended in the Fayerweather and Bromfield families of Boston. Several of the seats are marked "Capn Fayerweather" for merchant John Fayerweather, who, like other Boston merchants of his day, purchased large quantities of less ornamented, standard chairs from Boston craftsmen, and then shipped them to other colonial ports for sale, particularly New York. Harbor shipping records show that Boston merchants transported more than one thousand chairs to New York alone between 1744 and 1748. Captain Fayerweather may have given this more ornate set of chairs to his daughter Margaret. Family tradition claims that Margaret Fayerweather Bromfield (fig. 13) embroidered the seat covers.

H. 98.4 cm, w. 55.9 cm, d. 52.1 cm
(H. 38¾ in., w. 22 in., d. 20½ in.)
Gift of Mrs. Jean Frederic Wagniere, in memory of her mother, Henrietta Slade Warner (Mrs. Henry Eldridge Warner) 68.839

Card table

Boston, Massachusetts, 1730–50
Mahogany, chestnut, eastern white pine, original
needlework top

Boston's conservative Puritan roots continued to hold
sway in the first half of the eighteenth century as
extensive legislation against such social vices as
alcohol, tobacco, gambling, and card playing made
evident. Despite such laws, the existence of this card
table and a small group of related examples made
between 1730 and 1750 proves that wealthy Bostonians of the time participated in these forbidden activities and reveals a move in the Massachusetts Bay
Colony toward a more secular society. This table and
its mate were originally owned by Peter Fanueil, one
of the city's most prominent merchants and the
builder of Boston's Fanueil Hall.

This piece's finely wrought needlework playing
surface—no doubt the handiwork of a young woman
—belies the small transgression that the table represents. The embroidered scene is a common one
derived from contemporary print sources; it depicts a
shepherdess resting on her elbow amid an abundance
of flora and fauna. As part of their schooling, girls of
affluent families were taught several genteel skills,
including drawing, letter writing, conversation, and
needlework. Large embroidered pictures were cherished as significant accomplishments, often framed
or mounted and kept as a reminder of a woman's girl-
hood. Thus, secular rebellion and the innocence of
young womanhood collide in this single piece of furniture.

H. 68.6 cm, w. 90.5 cm, d. 89.3 cm
(H. 27 in., w. 35⅝ in., d. 35⅛ in.)
Anonymous contribution and Income of William E. Nickerson
Fund 49.330

Tilt-top tea table

Philadelphia, Pennsylvania, about 1760–75
Mahogany

Developed in the early eighteenth century, tilt-top tea tables are composed of a central pillar and three curved legs that support a round top. When not in use, the top can be tilted vertically. The tilting mechanism on more sophisticated examples allows for the table-top to swivel while horizontal as well. This adaptable design permitted hostesses to serve tea without reaching, or to store the table against a wall while still exhibiting its craftsmanship and beauty.

Utility alone, however, did not make these tables so fashionable. The advent of tea parties, which brought men and women together in an informal setting for spirited conversation (and often juicy gossip), made the tea table a necessary accoutrement for every society hostess. Drinking tea seated at a round tea table increased interaction between the sexes and offered newcomers an easy entree into society. Unspoken, yet socially important rules of gentility were often dubbed "tea-table decorum," suggesting that the object itself epitomized the politeness of the society that gathered around it.

These rules of refinement were increasingly emphasized by the elite as a way to distinguish themselves from the growing masses who could afford plain versions of such luxury goods. The main structural elements of a tea table (turned top, turned pillar, and carved legs) could be made in mass quantities, and unadorned tables were sold at modest prices to the midlevel market. As embellishments were added, the price increased, and so this fine Philadelphia example must have been very expensive. The elaborate and robust carving is attributed to one of the city's most skilled artisans of the period. While this craftsman's work is well known, his identity remains a mystery.

H. 75.9 cm, diam. top 84.8 cm (H. 29⅞ in., diam. top 33⅜ in.)
The M. and M. Karolik Collection of Eighteenth-Century
American Arts 39.146

Dressing table

Philadelphia, Pennsylvania, about 1760–70
San Domingo mahogany, mahogany veneer, yellow
poplar, cedar

Figural motifs, such as the delicate swan carved on the central drawer of this Philadelphia dressing table, are rare on American furniture. This table belongs to a small group of Philadelphia Rococo pieces embellished with decoration thought to represent various scenes from Aesop's *Fables*. The popularity of Aesop's tales soared in the mid-eighteenth century. At least three editions were published by Philadelphia printers in 1777 alone, and illustrations from the stories were widely copied by English and American craftsmen on textiles, architectural carving, and other media. The irony that these moralistic stories warning against greed, vanity, and other vices were used to embellish expensive luxury goods did not seem to bother eighteenth-century consumers.

Although several furniture design books incorporated Aesop's fables, the carving on the group to which this table belongs relates directly to illustrations in Thomas Johnson's *One Hundred and Fifty New Designs,* published in London in 1761. Johnson mixed imagery from Aesop's stories with chinoiserie and French Rococo motifs. Examples of each ornament the MFA's dressing table: chinoiserie fretwork in the cornice molding, flowering vines on the quarter columns, and a playful string of rocaille C-scrolls outlining the skirt. The focal point, however, is the central drawer, where the majestic swan swims above dripping rocaille rock forms amid a dizzying arrangement of C-scrolls and chinoiserie columns.

H. 81 cm, w. 92.1 cm, d. 51.8 cm
(H. 31⅞ in., w. 36¼ in., d. 20⅜ in.)
The M. and M. Karolik Collection of Eighteenth-Century
American Arts 39.150

Bread basket

Daniel Christian Fueter (1720–1785)

New York, New York, about 1765

Silver

Daniel Christian Fueter's extraordinary silver bread basket is one of the most sophisticated examples of Rococo silver made in the American colonies. Simultaneously light and monumental, the basket is a tour de force of design and technique. The delicate, lacy openwork lends a sense of liveliness as light plays on the reflecting solids and through the voids of the pierced body, and yet the seemingly whimsical pattern is tightly controlled in execution and further contained by a solid, cast border of undulating fruit and foliage. All of the cast, or molded, elements—the detailed and pierced border, scrolled feet, and twisted handle with unusual female masks—defy the solidity of their structure and add to the curving movement of the work.

Fueter, born and trained in Switzerland, arrived in New York with his family in 1754 after fleeing from Bern because of his involvement in a failed plot to overthrow the local government. He made this basket for Richard Harrison, whose family's coat of arms is engraved on the interior. The basket was most likely created about the time of Harrison's graduation from Columbia University in 1764, before Fueter left the city to pursue a three-year, ill-fated mining venture in Connecticut. Harrison undoubtedly came from a family of wealth and power, as few young men could afford such an extravagant luxury. Later in life, Harrison served his country as a delegate to the New York constitutional convention of 1788, and in 1789 was appointed by George Washington to be the first U.S. district attorney.

H. 27.1 cm, w. 37.8 cm, d. 31.1 cm, wt. 1866.2 gm
(H. 10¹¹⁄₁₆ in., w. 14⅞ in., d. 12¼ in., wt. 60 oz.)
Decorative Arts Special Fund   54.857

Fireback

Joseph Webb (about 1734–1787)

Boston, Massachusetts, about 1770–87

Cast iron

Made of durable cast iron, firebacks protected the rear wall of the fireplace from damaging flames and heat. Because of their prominent and highly visible location in the hearth, the source of light and warmth for many household activities, they were often embellished in the latest styles or with a family's crest. On this example, the florid Rococo border of C-scrolls and acanthus leaves is closely related to furniture and architectural decoration of the era. The same woodcarvers who embellished high chests and chairs often carved the wooden molds used to create firebacks.

Amid the leafy flourish, this fireback bears the arms of the Grand Lodge of the Freemasons in Massachusetts—three castles, and an open compass surmounted by a dove carrying an olive branch. The Freemasons, a secretive, philosophical brotherhood of artisans and merchants, were quite active in the American colonies, particularly in Boston, where their meetings were a hotbed of revolutionary thought

in the 1760s and early 1770s. Patriot and silversmith Paul Revere was a prominent Freemason who belonged to the same lodge as the Joseph Webb named in this fireback's lower inscription: "SOLD BY JOSEPH WEBB BOSTON." Revere even engraved a trade card for Webb in 1765 that advertised "All Sorts of Cast Iron work, done in ye best Manner," including "Chimney Backs of all Sizes." Revere and Webb's lodge, Saint Anthony's, met at the Green Dragon Tavern, renamed the Free Mason's Arms in 1764. The inscription at the top of the fireback, "THE•FREE•MASONS•ARMS," may refer to the crest it surmounts, or to the tavern where this influential group of Bostonians met on a regular basis.

H. 64.1 cm, w. 68.6 cm, d. 3.8 cm (H. 25¼ in., w. 27 in., d. 1½ in.)

Gift of a Friend of the Department of American Decorative Arts and Sculpture, William N. Banks Foundation, John Walton, Inc., and Edwin E. Jack Fund   1982.618

Desk and bookcase

George Bright (1726–1805)

Boston, Massachusetts, about 1770–85
Mahogany, white pine, glass

This mahogany desk and bookcase represents the pinnacle of the Rococo style in
Boston. When ornamenting their furniture,
Boston craftsmen and their clients were
often more reserved than their counterparts
in New York and Philadelphia, but this piece
defies that tendency. The shape of the piece
itself is decorative with a swelled lower
case, a design called "bombé." Standing on
vigorously carved cabriole (curved) legs and
claw-and-ball feet, this lower case contains
four long drawers and a slant-front desk.
The desk's interior compartments are composed of subtly shaped drawers and carved
fans. Instead of solid wood, the doors are
adorned with reflective mirrors set in
carved and gilt scalloped borders. The doors
are flanked by carved fluted pilasters
topped by Ionic capitals. A brilliant gilt
eagle perched above a broken scroll pediment and magnificently carved rosettes
with delicate cascading tendrils represent a
lavish level of ornamentation unparalleled
in Boston furniture.

This masterpiece is signed on one of its
drawers by George Bright, a successful
Boston cabinetmaker whom one customer
described in 1787 as "the neatest workman in
town." Despite his strong reputation during
his lifetime, Bright's work was unknown
until this signature was discovered by MFA
curators in the early 1960s, several years after it came
into the Museum's collection. The craftsman made the
piece for Judge Samuel Barrett of Boston, who presented it to his daughter Ann upon her marriage to Dr.
Isaac Green of Vermont. The Greens placed the desk
and bookcase in the front parlor of their Vermont
home in 1792, and it remained there until it was
bequeathed to the MFA by a descendant in 1956.

H. 252.7 cm, w. 109.2 cm, d. 61 cm
(H. 99½ in., w. 43 in., d. 24 in.)
Bequest of Miss Charlotte Hazen 56.1194

Desk and bookcase

Newport, Rhode Island, 1760–75
San Domingo mahogany, chestnut,
pine, cherry

This desk and bookcase features a
blockfront design consisting of vertical convex panels flanking a concave
panel on its base, slant lid, and bookcase. The panels on the slant lid and
bookcase doors are capped with cor-
responding convex and concave
carved shells. This alternating shell
motif is a signature feature of mid-
eighteenth-century Newport furniture and an exclusively American
design.

The innovative and refined embellishment, quality materials (even the
hidden interior elements are often
made of expensive mahogany), skill
and precision of the craftsmanship,
and attention to detail of Newport
block-and-shell furniture rate it
among the finest furniture made in
colonial America. Even in their own
time, Newport cabinetmakers were
known throughout the colonies, as
the entrepreneurial craftsmen
aggressively sold their wares in other
coastal cities via the active intercolo-
nial shipping network. The signature
shell motif was copied elsewhere, but
the imitators never reached the
sophistication of design or quality of
execution of the Newport manner.

H. 241.9 cm, w. 101.3 cm, d. 66 cm
(H. 95¼ in., w. 39⅞ in., d. 26 in.)
The M. and M. Karolik Collection of
Eighteenth-Century American Arts
39.155

Coffeepot and salver

Richard Humphreys (1749–1832)

Philadelphia, Pennsylvania, about 1770–80

Silver

This majestic coffeepot is among the best Rococo silver produced in Philadelphia. The double-bellied form, gadrooned borders on the foot and lid, and scrolled, curving spout are characteristic hallmarks of the style, but perhaps the most beautiful passage of the object is on the side: the coat of arms and crest of a horse engraved within a delicate shell and foliate cartouche. The accompanying salver is supported on claw-and-ball feet and is engraved with the same coat of arms at its center. Shown here as a support for the coffeepot, it could also have been used as a server or stand for a single teacup, saucer, and spoon. Fashioning stands en suite with teapots and coffeepots seems to have been common in Philadelphia, although the custom is rarely encountered elsewhere in American silver.

The talented Quaker silversmith Richard Humphreys was born in Tortola in the British West Indies. Apprenticed to Bancroft Woodcock in Wilmington, Delaware, he opened his own shop in Philadelphia in 1772. Although a relatively small number of objects by him are known, each—like this coffeepot and salver—is extraordinary. After service in the Revolution (for which he was censured by the Quaker Friends), he resumed his craft at "The Sign of the Coffee Pot" on Front Street in 1781 and later at different locations. He is perhaps best known as the maker of a large Neoclassical urn presented to Charles Thomson by the Continental Congress in 1774, when he was elected secretary of that political body, a position he held until 1789. That urn is engraved by James Smither, who may have executed the engraving here.

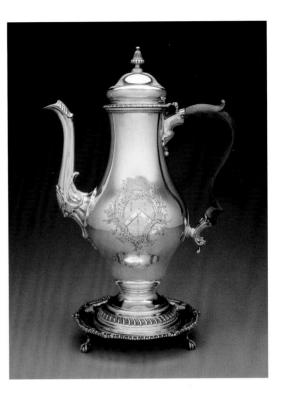

Coffeepot: H. 34.4 cm, diam. base 11.4 cm, wt. 1202.9 gm
(H. 13⁹/₁₆ in., diam. base 4½ in., wt. 38 oz. 13 dwt. 12 gr.)
Salver: H. 3.8 cm, diam. 16.9 cm, wt. 300.1 gm
(H. 1½ in., diam. 6¹¹/₁₆ in., wt. 9 oz. 13 dwt.)
Gift in memory of Dr. George Clymer by his wife, Mrs. Clymer
56.589–590

 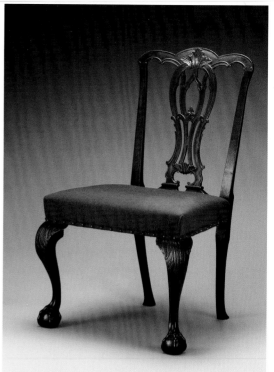

Side chair

Boston, Massachusetts, about 1765–85

Mahogany, soft maple, red oak

H. 97.2 cm, w. 62.5 cm, d. 47.9 cm

(H. 38¼ in., w. 24⅝ in., d. 18⅞ in.)

Gift of Priscilla Quincy Weld in memory of her mother and grandmother, Ruth Draper Peters and Alice Ames Draper and Elizabeth M. and John F. Paramino Fund, Arthur Tracy Cabot Fund, Ernest Kahn Fund, John Wheelock Elliott and John Morse Elliott Fund, Alice M. Bartlett Fund, and Edwin E. Jack Fund   1996.52

Side chair

Boston, Massachusetts, about 1770

Mahogany, maple, pine

H. 93.3 cm, w. 56.5 cm, d. 45.7 cm

(H. 36¾ in., w. 22¼ in., d. 18 in.)

Museum purchase with funds by exchange from Gift of Mary W. Bartol, John W. Bartol, and Abigail W. Clark, Gift of Dr. and Mrs. Thomas H. Weller, Bequest of Mrs. Stephen S. FitzGerald, Bequest of Dr. Samuel A. Green, Gift of Gilbert L. Steward, Jr., Gift of Mrs. Daniel Risdon, Gift of Miss Elizabeth Clark in memory of Mary R. Crowninshield, Gift of Mrs. Clark McIlwaine, Gift of Mr. and Mrs. Russell W. Knight — Collection of Ralph E. and Myra T. Tibbetts, Gift of Elizabeth Shapleigh, Gift of Miss Harriet A. Robeson, Gift of the John Gardner Greene Estate, Bequest of Barbara Boylston Bean, Gift of Miss Catherine W. Faucon, Gift of Jerrold H. Barnett and Joni Evans Barnett, and Gift of Dr. Martha M. Eliot 2004.2062

The exuberant Rococo style flourished almost simultaneously in England and her American colonies. These two roughly contemporary chairs, both made in Boston, illustrate two primary means of the style's transfer and cultural diffusion: imported objects and printed designs.

The first chair, shown to the left and one of a large set, was once owned by Moses Gill, a wealthy hardware merchant in Boston and Princeton, Massachusetts. Through his business and social connections in the city and political activity leading up to the Revolution, Gill may have known William Phillips, a fellow Boston merchant who owned a strikingly similar chair that had been imported from London (fig. 14). Although the proportions, secondary woods, and quality of the carving differ, the same intricate, ribbonlike seat back, stop-fluted rear posts, and unusual hairy-paw feet of both chairs suggests that the American example was made by someone who had access to, or was familiar with, the London chair.

Engraved furniture designs published during the 1750s and 1760s spread the Rococo style even more quickly and to a greater audience than did the copying of specific models. The second Boston chair, illustrated to the right, with its Gothic-arched seat back design, is based directly on plate 14 of Thomas Chippendale's famous *Gentleman and Cabinet-Maker's Director* of 1762 (fig. 15). Although copies of the *Director* were owned in New England, few examples of the region's surviving furniture relate closely to the book's designs. This chair is therefore an important and rare document of the influence of imported pattern and design books on Boston furniture.

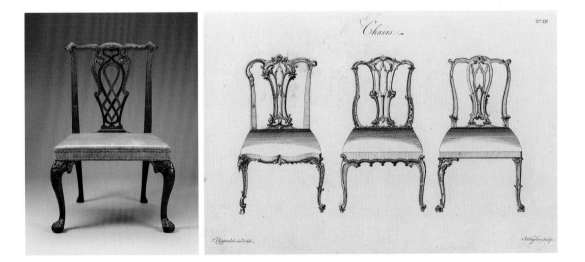

fig. 14. (above left) **Side chair, Thomas Hooper (active about 1750), England, about 1750–60.** fig. 15. (above right) **"Chairs" (detail), from Thomas Chippendale, *The Gentleman and Cabinet-Maker's Director,* 1762, plate 14.**

Cathedra (bishop's chair)

Probably Puebla, Mexico, about 1760–1800
Spanish cedar, modern leather upholstery with original
and reproduction brass nails

Just as craftsmen in Britain's thirteen American colonies developed their own regional interpretations of the Rococo style, so did Spanish colonists living in Central and South America. While furniture makers in Philadelphia, Boston, New York, and Charleston largely followed British precedents, craftsmen in Mexico took their cue from Spanish fashions. In general, the Spanish Rococo style was bolder and more exaggerated than British interpretations. Those characteristics hold true for the work of its colonists as well.

This massive armchair possesses many signature Rococo characteristics, including scrolled arms and ears, elaborate foliate carving, masks ornamenting the knees, and enormous claw-and-ball feet. The heavy, almost aggressive design is an even further exaggeration of the Spanish Rococo. Called a cathedra, or bishop's chair, the armchair was probably made for use in a Catholic church in Puebla, a Spanish port established in 1531. Its overall sculptural form and strong presence demand attention and reverence fitting for its use in a church. The thronelike chair is carved on all sides, including an elaborate sun effigy on the outside of the chair back.

H. 111.8 cm, w. 58.4 cm, d. 93.9 cm
(H. 44 in., w. 23 in., d. 37 in.)
Gift of Landon T. Clay and Harriet Otis Cruft Fund   1980.171

Teapot

Paul Revere Jr. (1734–1818)

Boston, Massachusetts, about 1760–65

Silver

Long before he earned fame as a zealous patriot, Paul Revere Jr. was well known among his contemporaries as a superb silversmith and engraver. He learned his trade from his father, Paul Revere Sr., who had emigrated from France as a young man and apprenticed with noted silversmith John Coney. The younger Revere inherited the shop after his father's death in 1754, working under his mother's name until he came of age a year later. The craftsman's early work shows his quick adoption and mastery of the Rococo style, both in engraving and three-dimensional works in silver.

This extraordinary teapot is one of the finest surviving Rococo teapots from Boston. The sophisticated double-bellied shape is embellished with raised, chased decoration, as opposed to the more common flat, engraved method. The designs, which were punched out from the interior of the piece, decorate the shoulder of the teapot and form the central cartouche. The iconography includes common

Rococo motifs such as C-scrolls, raffles (ruffle-like decoration), and a variety of flowers arranged in an energetic and asymmetrical fashion, as well as a more exotic bird and chinoiserie pavilion. These unusual motifs indicate Revere's advanced knowledge of, and willingness to experiment with, the Rococo style.

H. 14.9 cm, diam. base 8.3 cm, wt. 658.1 gm (H. 5⅞ in., diam. base 3¼ in., wt. 21 oz. 3 dwt. 12 gr.)
Pauline Revere Thayer Collection 35.1775

fig. 16. **John Singleton Copley** (1738–1815), *Paul Revere*, Boston, Massachusetts, 1768.

Sons of Liberty Bowl

Paul Revere Jr. (1734–1818)

Boston, Massachusetts, 1768

Silver

Inscription: "To the Memory of the glorious NINETY-TWO: Members / of the Hon^bl House of Representatives of the Massachusetts-Bay; / who, undaunted by the insolent Menaces of Villains in Power, / from a Strict Regard to Conscience, and the LIBERTIES / of their Constituents, on the 30th of June 1768, / Voted NOT TO RESCIND."

This simple punch bowl is one of the most celebrated and imitated examples of colonial American silver. Its reputation is not based on any unique aspect of its style or form, which is derived from imported Chinese porcelain bowls, but on the cause it commemorates: the struggle for American independence.

The "Liberty Bowl" honors ninety-two members of the Massachusetts House of Representatives who refused to rescind their letter sent throughout the colonies protesting the Townshend Acts of 1767, which taxed tea, paper, glass, and other commodities

imported from England. This act of civil disobedience by the "Glorious Ninety-Two" was the first public act of rebellion against the British crown and a major step leading to the American Revolution.

Patriot and silversmith Paul Revere was commissioned to make the bowl by fifteen members of the Sons of Liberty, a secret organization to which Revere belonged. The names of these fifteen men are boldly engraved on the bowl's rim. The defiant inscription uses incendiary language probably composed by fellow society member Dr. Joseph Warren.

Other engraved symbols include references to Englishman John Wilkes, whose published writings in defense of liberty decried government violations of the Magna Carta and the Bill of Rights. Wilkes's words infuriated the Crown but became a rallying cry for American patriots, for whom "No. 45," the issue number of the *North Briton* in which Wilkes's most famous article appeared, and "Wilkes and Liberty" were potent symbols. The Sons of Liberty used the bowl to serve punch at their clandestine meetings; John Rowe's diary account on August 1, 1768, suggests that they may have called the bowl "No. 45": "Spent the evening at Mr. Barber's Insurance Office & the Silver Bowl was this evening for the first time introduced, No. 45. Weighs 45 ounces & holds 45 gills...." Symbolic even in weight and size, the bowl held 45 gills of rum punch, the beverage preferred by colonists during the boycott of government-taxed tea.

The Liberty Bowl, the Declaration of Independence, and the Constitution have been called the nation's most cherished historical treasures. The MFA purchased the bowl in 1949 with funds that included seven hundred donations by Boston schoolchildren and the general public.

H. 13.9 cm, diam. base 14.8 cm, diam. rim 27.9 cm, wt. 1363.1 gm (H. 5½ in., diam. base 5¹³⁄₁₆ in., diam. rim 11 in., wt. 43 oz. 16 dwt. 12 gr.)
Gift by Subscription and Francis Bartlett Fund 49.45

Fruit basket

The American China Manufactury (active 1770–1772)
of Gousse Bonnin (about 1741–1780)
and George Anthony Morris (1742/5–1773)

Philadelphia, Pennsylvania, 1771–72
Soft-paste porcelain with underglaze blue decoration

The American China Manufactory was the first and only successful porcelain factory in the colonies. Erected in Philadelphia with great fanfare, Gousse Bonnin and George Anthony Morris's factory produced its first batch in late 1770. At the time, it appeared to have a bright future: the rebellious Nonimportation Agreements of the 1760s encouraged American manufacturers to supplant British imports, such prominent Philadelphia intellectuals as Benjamin Franklin supported the scientific effort to produce the elusive luxury goods, and skilled porcelain workers were successfully recruited from overseas.

The American China Manufactory produced all sorts of tablewares, from plates and tea cups to more ambitious forms, such as this pierced fruit basket. Its products were nearly identical to those of English factories in Bow and Lowestoft in both form and decoration, but the American company's porcelains did not maintain a consistent high quality, often varying in materials and execution. For example, the surface of this basket has a less desirable, gritty texture from impurities in the glaze, and the underglaze blue decoration is blurred on the rim and side walls.

Ironically, despite the factory's patriotic origins, this basket was owned by Daniel Whitehead, a Philadelphia loyalist who later had to forfeit his property during the Revolution; he retained the basket, however, and it descended in his family until it was acquired by the Museum. It is one of only twenty or so American China Manufactory works known to survive today.

Although Bonnin and Morris's porcelain adorned the most fashionable Philadelphia tables, their business venture failed in less than two years. The factory could not compete with the flood of cheap imports that continued to enter American ports regardless of the patriotic support espoused, but perhaps not practiced, by many.

H. 6.8 cm, diam. 17.5 cm
(H. 2¹¹⁄₁₆ in., diam. 6⁷⁄₈ in.)
Frederick Brown Fund
1977.621

Covered goblet (*pokal*)

Attributed to the New Bremen Glass Manufactory
(active 1784–1795) of John Frederick Amelung
(1741–1798)

Frederick County, Maryland, about 1785–95
Nonlead glass, free blown

Although glassmaking in early America began in the
seventeenth century at a variety of locations, technical difficulties and England's mercantile policy prevented it from flourishing. In the eighteenth century,
German immigrants Caspar Wistar and Henry
William Stiegel started successful glasshouses in
New Jersey and Pennsylvania, respectively, using
skilled workmen imported from Germany. However,
most window and table glass used in the colonies
continued to be imported from England.

Another German immigrant, Johann Frederick
Amelung, arrived in Maryland in 1784 with many
skilled workmen, technical expertise, and financial
backing from merchants in his hometown of Bremen.
For the next decade, Amelung's New Bremen factory—
perhaps the largest industrial enterprise in the country at the time—produced some of the most beautiful
and ambitious glass objects created in eighteenth-
century America, including many engraved presentation pieces for a distinguished clientele. Despite this
artistic success, New Bremen was forced into bank-
ruptcy, undermined by the vast influx of inexpensive
English glass in the post-Revolutionary economy.

This goblet is closely related in its form and chem-
ical composition to documented New Bremen work.
Bold in silhouette, with a large, easily grasped knop
between the flaring bowl and substantial, domed
foot, the goblet has a strong, almost visceral, presence that belies its inherent fragility. It was probably
used by the Evangelical Reformed and Lutheran con-
gregation of Bender's Church, established in 1781 in
Biglerville, Pennsylvania, only about forty miles
north of New Bremen.

H. 32.4 cm, diam. 11.4 cm (H. 12⅜ in., diam. 4½ in.)
Gift of The Seminarians and Mr. and Mrs. Daniel F. Morley
1994.82a–b

Chest-on-chest

John Cogswell (1738–1818)
Boston, Massachusetts, 1782
Mahogany, white pine

According to tradition, the wealthy merchant Elias Hasket Derby of Salem and his wife commissioned this chest-on-chest from John Cogswell in 1782 for their grandson John to take to Harvard College (for another example of the Derby's commissions, see page 95). The Derbys purchased lavish and monumental furniture for several of their children, and undoubtedly placed the order for this piece to be in the latest fashion. Cogswell, an established and well-respected Boston cabinetmaker, fulfilled that desire with one of the most sophisticated furniture shapes made in the colonies, the bombé.

The bombé shape, characterized by a swelled lower section and based upon scattered European precedents, was almost exclusively made in the colonies in Boston and Salem, Massachusetts. Unlike their peers in Philadelphia, who updated their style by adding flashy Rococo ornament to existing forms, Boston craftsmen experimented with the shape itself. Although many early bombé pieces were made of thick sides with curved exterior walls and straight inner walls and drawers, the drawers on this example follow the curve—a more elegant, but labor-intensive and costly method of construction. To create this shape, Cogswell (or a member of his shop) hollowed out the inner surface with chisels and large gouges, then extended and curved the drawer ends to exaggerate the effect. Cogswell continued to experiment with the bombé shape, and in later years maximized the sinuous motion of the form by adding undulating movement to the front of the case as well.

This chest-on-chest is further embellished with carved fretwork, or borders of geometric designs, rocaille appliqué, and urn and flame finials. The latter may have been made in the noted Skillin family workshop in Boston, operated sequentially by brothers John and Simeon Skillin.

Presumably proud of this piece, Cogswell signed it boldly on the top of the lower section: "Made By John / Cogswell in middle Street / Boston 1782." As the only known work with his full signature, this chest-on-chest serves as the benchmark for attributions to this innovative colonial craftsman.

H. 246.4 cm, w. 112.4 cm, d. 59.7 cm
(H. 97 in., w. 44¼ in., d. 23½ in.)
William Francis Warden Fund   1973.289

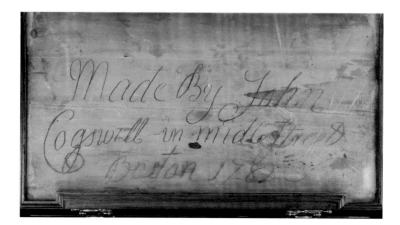

Neoclassicism and the New Nation: The Late Eighteenth and Early Nineteenth Centuries

Gerald W. R. Ward

In the decades following the Revolution, an expanding territory and an increasing population created lucrative markets for American craftsmen, who nevertheless continued to battle against a flood of English and Continental imports. Direct trade with China, inaugurated in the mid 1780s, also brought a wealth of imported porcelain and other wares to the new republic, but American artisans responded to the challenges presented by these conditions and produced extraordinary goods for their local clientele.

Classicism permeated almost every aspect of life and thought in America. Its impact was felt in government, education, architecture, and dress, as well as in furnishings, as citizens sought to emulate and recapture the virtues of the ancient Greeks and the republic of Rome. Although classical motifs had been part of the American design vocabulary since the seventeenth century, archaeological excavations in Herculaneum, Pompeii, and elsewhere in Europe in the mid-eighteenth century reawakened and deepened interest in the distant past. Stylistically, American work drew its primary inspiration from the art and architecture of ancient Greece and Rome, principally as interpreted through the pattern books and builder's guides of English architects and craftsmen, including Robert Adam, Thomas Sheraton, and George Hepplewhite, followed by Thomas Hope, George Smith, and others. French influence, which often (although not always) filtered through England before reaching the United States, was also a powerful component in the international movement now known as Neoclassicism. The more widespread use of printed sources began to

fig. 17. **Parlor from Oak Hill, South Danvers, Massachusetts, about 1800–1801, as installed at the Museum of Fine Arts, Boston; design and carving attributed to Samuel McIntire (1757–1811). Photograph © Lou Jones 1999.**

fig. 18. **Henry Sargent** (1770–1845),

The Dinner Party, Boston,

Massachusetts, about 1821.

blur the edges of the distinct regional styles prevalent in the colonial period, although differences among the work of various urban centers remain discernible.

Furniture and silver produced during the early phase of Neoclassicism, often referred to as the Federal period (about 1790 to 1820), are on the whole relatively light, delicate, and rectilinear, decorated with two-dimensional ornament such as inlay in furniture or bright-cutting (an ornamental technique in which the surface of silver is notched or gouged so as to form facets) in silver. Eagles, urns, and columns were among the dominant motifs. Elizabeth Derby West acquired objects of many kinds in this style for her magnificent mansion called Oak Hill, built about 1800–1801 in South Danvers, Massachusetts, and undoubtedly designed by Samuel McIntire of Salem. Three rooms from Oak Hill (fig. 17) , now preserved at the MFA, provide a rare opportunity to see high-style interiors of this period decorated with their original furniture and furnishings.

fig. 19. **Henry Sargent** (1770–1845),

The Tea Party, Boston,

Massachusetts, 1824.

Later Neoclassical objects, from about 1815 into the 1830s, are often more literal interpretations of antiquity and are usually termed Empire in style (after the first French Empire of 1804–1815). Monumental in scale, varied in materials, and with ornament derived from ancient Greek, Roman, and occasionally Egyptian sources, they also reflect a complex blend of contemporary French and English influences, as evident in the desk and bookcase by Anthony Quervelle of Philadelphia.

The Boston interiors depicted by Henry Sargent (which are probably rooms in the fashionable urban houses known as the Tontine Crescent designed by architect Charles Bulfinch) offer rare glimpses into the modes of arrangement, floor and window treatments, lighting, and social customs of this period. Although Sargent painted the two works at nearly the same time, the sideboard and other objects in *The Dinner Party* (fig. 18) are largely in the Federal style, while the parlors depicted in *The Tea Party* (fig. 19) are outfitted in the Empire mode.

Although American citizens of this period looked to the distant past for aesthetic inspiration, they also took nascent steps in the forward-focused transformation from craft to industry. Labor-saving devices and new materials became available in the production of silver, furniture, ceramics, glass, and other objects. In silversmithing, for example, rolled sheet silver began to be widely available early in this period. This allowed artisans to make vessels with considerably less time and effort than was required when raising a pot from an ingot with repeated hammer blows. Later, die-stamped bands of ornament, made in long strips and then easily soldered to the bodies of objects, and other machine-assisted techniques also facilitated and streamlined the process. In furniture, the production of standardized parts, such as chair components and turned table legs, helped with economies of scale, as shops became larger and contained more internal subdivisions. These changes in production methods were accompanied by changes in labor relations; so-called price books came into common usage in this period, establishing the wages to be paid by masters to journeymen for each task involved in chair- and cabinetmaking.

The national push to develop the country's manufacturing abilities resulted in the first economically successful attempts at producing porcelain in the United States at the Tucker factory in Philadelphia (fig. 20) and in significant developments in the glass industry in New England, Pittsburgh, West Virginia, and Ohio. These early efforts did little to diminish the dominance of English imports to the American market, but they set the stage for future development of the ceramics and glass industries in the United States.

Like their industry-focused contemporaries, American sculptors and their patrons sought to push their art to new levels. While woodcarvers and stonecarvers had reached high levels of proficiency in the seventeenth and eighteenth centuries, there was no market for traditional sculpture in America until the early nineteenth century. Pioneering sculptors of the early republic sought to master European themes and ancient techniques through the creation of images in white marble. Some, including Horatio Greenough and Thomas Crawford, traveled to Italy and spent much of their careers there, producing Neoclassical portraits, allegories, and literary subjects.

Neoclassicism was the first of many successive yet overlapping revival styles that would come to typify the eclecticism of the nineteenth century. While many of the later revivals were similarly linked to moralistic leanings or social movements, none captured the imagination and profoundly influenced the shape and look of the entire country to the extent of Neoclassicism.

fig. 20. (opposite) Pitcher, William Ellis Tucker Factory Porcelain Company (active 1826–1838), Philadelphia, Pennsylvania, about 1830.

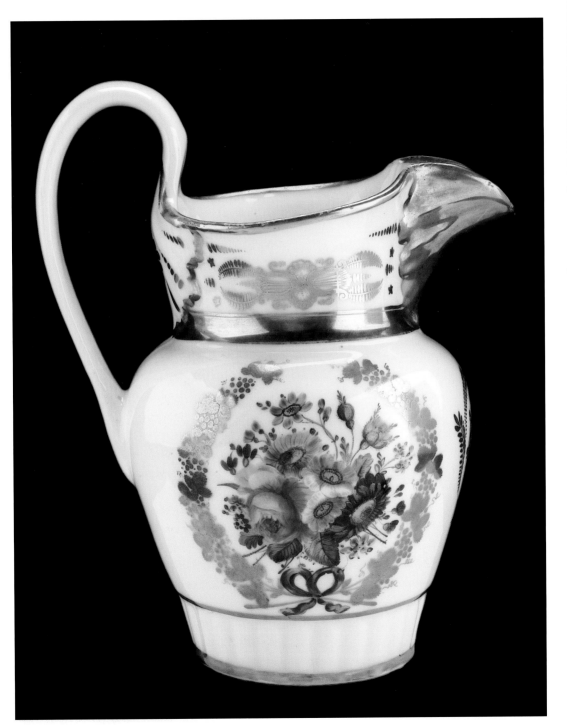

Chest-on-chest

Samuel McIntire (1757–1811), designer and carver;
central allegorical figure by a member of the
workshop operated by John Skillin (1745–1800)
or Simeon Skillin Jr. (1756–1806)
Salem, Massachusetts, about 1795–1805
Mahogany, mahogany veneer, light- and dark-wood
inlay, pine

This chest-on-chest—the most extraordinary and
spectacular of the furniture commissions by Salem
merchant Elias Hasket Derby and his wife—was
probably made for their daughter, Elizabeth, who
married Nathaniel West in 1783.

Most of the superb carving on the piece is attributed to Samuel McIntire, the Salem architect and
carver. For many years, the chest has been linked to
a bill from McIntire to Elizabeth Derby West, dated
1796 and specifying £3.3.0 worth of carving for a "Case
Drawers" made by a Mr. Lemon. The Museum's chest-
on-chest, however, includes much more carving than
the bill itemizes, and in style it closely resembles
McIntire's work from a wide time span. The cornu-
copia, baskets of fruit, flower vases, grapes, draped
putti, and other ornaments that enrich the top, bottom, and sides of the piece are similar to McIntire's
mature carving style found on furniture and interiors
from 1793 to 1805 or later, including Oak Hill, built
about 1800–1801 for Elizabeth Derby West, and the
Gardner-Pingree house in Salem, built about 1804.

Standing proudly atop this masterpiece is a rare
allegorical figure, interpreted by scholars variously
as representing Nike or the virtues of the new America. She clutches a laurel wreath in her right hand and
a pike in her left, and her bosom is ornamented with a
golden sun. Based on a close analysis of its style and
workmanship, the figure is currently attributed to a
journeyman in the noted Boston workshop operated
by the Skillin family of shipcarvers.

H. 260.4 cm, w. 118.7 cm, d. 60.9 cm
(H. 102½ in., w. 46¾ in., d. 24 in.)
The M. and M. Karolik Collection of Eighteenth-Century
American Arts 41.580

Lady's writing table with tambour shutters

John Seymour and Son (active 1794–1816)
Boston, Massachusetts, about 1796–98
Satinwood veneer, eastern white pine, black ash, cedar,
cherry, black walnut, and light- and dark-wood inlays

John Seymour and his son, Thomas, were the premier cabinetmakers in Federal-period Boston. Born and trained in England, they came to Massachusetts via Portland, Maine, in the early 1790s and began producing stylish Neoclassical furniture for the local clientele. Of their large production, however, few pieces are marked, labeled, or otherwise signed. This stunning satinwood desk, made shortly after the Seymours' arrival in Boston, is notable for its fine

craftsmanship, carefully selected woods, and elegant design. Moreover, it fortuitously retains its original paper label pasted to the outside of the backboard, giving the name of the firm and advertising its location on Creek Square in Boston.

The form was known in its own day as a "lady's writing table with tambour shutters"; today it is normally called a tambour desk because of its use of tambour doors enclosing the interior in the upper case. These doors consist of strips of satinwood glued vertically to a linen backcloth, and each shutter then slides in a groove that runs across the front, sides, and part of the back of the upper case, allowing access, when in the open position, to the twelve small drawers and six pigeonholes that form the functional spaces of the interior. Each pigeonhole, meant to hold folded correspondence and other documents, is fitted with a Gothic arch and has a blue-painted interior. Tambour desks, a novel form in the Federal period, were specifically made for women and were especially popular in New England, reflecting the region's emphasis on reading, writing, and female education in the early years of the new republic.

H. 128.3 cm, w. 100.9 cm, d. 51.1 cm
(H. 50½ in., w. 39¾ in., d. 20⅛ in.)
Museum purchase with funds donated
anonymously and Henry H. and Zoë Oliver
Sherman Fund   2000.636

Teapot
Paul Revere Jr. (1734–1818)
Boston, Massachusetts, 1796
Silver

After a hiatus in his silversmithing business during the Revolution, Paul Revere returned to his craft about 1780. Soon his shop began producing silver in the newest taste, using the latest technology. This fluted teapot, for example, is probably based on similar English works in silver, fused plate (also called Sheffield plate), or ceramic wares, and it is made of rolled sheet silver. Bending sheets of thin silver, produced in rolling mills, into a desired form and soldering them together took less time and effort than the traditional, more laborious method of raising a vessel from an ingot with repeated hammer blows. Here, Revere decorated the teapot with dotted and bright-cut bands over tasseled festoons at top and bottom, all in the latest Neoclassical style.

Revere entered a charge for this teapot in his account book on June 18, 1796, noting its sale to Jonathan Hunnewell, a mason and distinguished citizen of Boston. As was common, the intrinsic value of the silver (at 7 shillings per ounce for a total value of £7.1.0) was roughly equivalent to the price Revere charged for making and engraving the vessel (£7.10.0), bringing the total cost to £14.11.0. Hunnewell also ordered a stand for the teapot and a sugar basket, twelve teaspoons, sugar tongs, and four salt shovels.

Hunnewell and Revere were friends. Each was an active member of the Massachusetts Charitable Mechanics Society, a mutual aid organization founded in 1795; Revere was the first president and Hunnewell the second.

H. 15.9 cm, w. 29.2 cm, wt. 643.8 gm
(H. 6¼ in., w. 11½ in., wt. 20 oz. 14 dwt.)
Pauline Revere Thayer Collection 35.1779

Five-piece tea and coffee set

Christian Wiltberger (1766–1851)

Philadelphia, Pennsylvania, about 1795

Silver

Christian Wiltberger, a second-generation German American, served his apprenticeship with Richard Humphreys of Philadelphia (see p. 75). The work of master and apprentice, while equally proficient, aptly demonstrates the stylistic shift from the Rococo mode to Neoclassicism. In this tea and coffee set by Wiltberger, the fluted, urn-shaped bodies of each of the five pieces demonstrate the Federal-period preference for this ancient form, as well as the custom—new in silver at this time—of fashioning tea sets in a conforming manner. The surface ornament is essentially two-dimensional; it is limited to engraving and bright-cut decoration, including a wide band of framed medallions enclosing a sunburst design that encircles the body of each object. Wiltberger, operating out of his shop near Christ Church in the 1790s, advertised that "he continues to carry on the Silver Smith and Jeweller's business in all its branches as

usual. He has also on hand a large and elegant assortment of Silver Plated Wares, Jewellery, &c. imported by the latest arrivals from Europe, together with a considerable quantity of silver ware manufactured immediately under his own inspection."

According to family tradition, Wiltberger created this service, consisting of a large coffeepot, teapot, creampot, sugar bowl, and slop (or waste) bowl, for Captain Bernard Raser and his wife Mary Raser, who married in 1795. Each piece bears their initials, "BMR," engraved in script within a wreath. The set descended in their family until it was given to the Museum in 1961.

Coffeepot: H. 35.6 cm, diam. base 10.8 cm, wt. 1161.7 gm
(H. 14 in., diam. base 4¼ in., wt. 37 oz. 7 dwt.)
Gift of John H. Farovid in memory of Bertha Sease Farovid, Mary Vincent Farovid, and Bishop John Heyl Vincent
61.949–953

Oval-back side chair

Philadelphia, Pennsylvania, or Salem, Massachusetts,
about 1795–1800

Beech, maple, oak

H. 98.4 cm, w. 55.2 cm, d. 48.3 cm
(H. 38¾ in., w. 21¾ in., d. 19 in.)

The M. and M. Karolik Collection of Eighteenth-Century
American Arts 39.108

Side chair

**Probably by Thomas Seymour (1771–1848); possibly
with John Seymour (1738–1818)**

Boston, Massachusetts, 1804–10

Mahogany, crotch-satinwood or birch veneer, birch

H. 88.9 cm, w. 48.3 cm, d. 40.6 cm
(H. 35 in., w. 19 in., d. 16 in.)

The M. and M. Karolik Collection of Eighteenth-Century
American Arts 41.610a

In the Federal period, illustrated pattern books and
price books began to play an increasingly significant
role as design sources for American cabinetmakers.
George Hepplewhite and Thomas Sheraton are perhaps the most familiar names today among
those who were published, but many
others were present in the libraries of
major cabinet shops of their era. For
example, the elegant side chair illustrated to the far right and attributed
to the Seymour shop of Boston, is
based on a design in the *London
Chair-Maker' and Carvers' Book of
Prices for Workmanship,* published
in 1802.

The Seymours brought this
design to life by playing light
satinwood or birch veneers
against dark mahogany.

Several passages of the chair, including the curving
crest rail with its carved, turned, and veneered elements, the delicate tracery of the back rails, and the
raking front legs, demonstrate their great technical
woodworking skills. The Seymours are the only
Boston shop known to have produced this complex
chair design, which they issued in several variations.

The painted oval-back chair on the left is modeled
after a pattern in the 1788 and 1789 editions of Hepplewhite's *Cabinet-Maker and Upholsterer's Guide;* the
design was omitted from the "improved" third edition
of 1794, presumably because it was outdated. Hepplewhite asserted that "a new and very elegant fashion
has arisen . . . , of finishing [chairs] with painted or
japanned work, which gives a rich and splendid
appearance to the minuter parts of the ornaments,
which are generally thrown in by the painter." Made
for the Derby family of Salem, Massachusetts, this
chair and numerous related examples have been
attributed to either Philadelphia, Pennsylvania, or
Salem; their origin remains unclear to this day.

Side chair

Samuel Gragg (1772–1855)

Boston, Massachusetts, about 1808–12

Painted ash, hickory

Experimentation in forms, materials, and techniques was a dominant theme in nineteenth-century American woodworking, as craftsmen and manufacturers sought to improve upon tradition. This side chair, which gives with the weight of a sitter but always returns to its original shape when unoccupied, is an early manifestation of this interest.

The chair's maker, Samuel Gragg, received a patent for an "elastic chair" on August 31, 1808. Gragg adapted the ancient practice of bending wood with moisture and heat to create his sinuous chairs in keeping with classical Greek forms, as interpreted through the latest English pattern books by Thomas Hope, George Smith, and others. Daringly, Gragg achieved the chair's striking compound-curve design by steaming a single piece of wood to serve as the rear upper post, or stile, seat rail, and front leg on each side. The back supports are similarly bold, as are the strongly raking rear legs, curved stretchers between the legs, and other elements that complete the elegant lines.

The decoration of the chair, probably executed by a specialist, is as fashionable as the construction is innovative. Painted a tawny color overall, the chair is accented with striping in shades of brown. The stiles have pendant green leaves at their apex, while the wider central back support is embellished with a skillfully painted, wispy peacock feather. In form and decoration, this chair represents an early manifestation of the "Fancy" style, popularized from 1790 to 1840 and characterized by attention-grabbing shapes and ornament inspired by the imagination.

H. 86.7 cm, w. 45.7 cm, d. 50.8 cm (H. 34⅛ in., w. 18 in., d. 20 in.)
Charles Hitchcock Tyler Residuary Fund   61.1074

Fall-front desk (*secrétaire à abbatant*)

Thomas Emmons and George Archibald (active 1813–1825)

Boston, Massachusetts, 1813–25

Mahogany veneer, mahogany

The firm of Thomas Emmons and George Archibald, active between 1813 and Emmons's death in 1825, was a leader in Boston furniture making in the years after the War of 1812. Worthy successors to John and Thomas Seymour, the partners produced fashionable mahogany furniture in the French Empire style, including this fall-front desk (or *secrétaire à abbatant*) bearing their stenciled label.

Made in the restrained French taste, this secretary is characteristic of the elegant nature of Emmons and Archibald's work and of Boston furniture in this period. Carefully selected mahogany veneers and superbly carved hairy-paw feet provide points of visual interest to the largely rectilinear, vertical form. Brass caps and bases accent the columns at each side of the case, while a floral escutcheon surrounds the lock on the fall-front. According to their advertisement in a Boston newspaper on June 1, 1825, the firm's stock-in-trade included "a variety of elegant French CAPS and BASES, Rings, Knobs, and other Ornaments" that may have been imported from France.

The Emmons and Archibald establishment at 39 Orange (later Washington) Street had a three-story warehouse, "commodiously arranged for exhibiting furniture," a thirteen-room dwelling house with yard and outbuildings, and "in the rear very extensive workshops with suitable fixtures and a large space protected from the sun for seasoning mahogany." The extent of the enterprise is indicated by the eleven workbenches located in the shop, where journeymen and apprentices labored at their tasks.

H. 153.7 cm, w. 97.8 cm, d. 49.5 cm (H. 60½ in., w. 38½ in., d. 19½ in.) Gift of a Friend of the Department and Otis Norcross Fund   1985.335

Commode

Thomas Seymour (1771–1848) **and James Cogswell**
(1780–1862); **painted by John Ritto Penniman**
(1782–1841); **probably carved by Thomas Wightman**
(**born about 1740**)
Boston, Massachusetts, 1809
Mahogany; mahogany, crotch-mahogany, crotch-birch,
rosewood, and bird's-eye-maple veneers; satinwood and
rosewood crossbanding; eastern white pine, white ash,
maple; brass

Thomas Seymour sold this spectacular commode to
Elizabeth Derby West, daughter of the wealthy merchant Elias Hasket Derby, for her home, Oak Hill, in
South Danvers, Massachusetts. The son of English
immigrant cabinetmaker John Seymour, Thomas
Seymour had strong connections to a network of
native and immigrant craftsmen. The commode was
the ambitious collaborative undertaking of highly
skilled artisans offering the finest level of materials
and craftsmanship available in Boston, rivaling any
in the United States.

Seymour's design is a sophisticated interpretation
of the English style. Although the bright, highly figured veneers are flamboyant, the form is restrained
and elegant. Shaped fronts were common on case furniture of this period, but the semielliptical plan of
this commode presented an unusual challenge. The
eight wedge-shaped side drawers swing open on
hinges, with no interior space wasted. Each one
added a considerable amount of work and expense,
demonstrating that Seymour lavished attention on
even the smallest details of construction, making this
piece one of the finest examples of his craft.

The commode's rounded top offered an opportunity for a showy radial display of contrasting
mahogany and birch veneers. The highlight, however,
is the design of seashells and leaves skillfully rendered by the decorative painter John Ritto Penniman.
A receipt dated 1809 documents the work: "Large
Mahogany Comode, [$]80.00. / Paid Mr. Penniman's
Bill, for Painting Shels on Top of Do [ditto] [$]10.00."
The crisp, confident carving of the blossoms at the
tops of the colonettes and the patterned lower edge of
the case is attributed to another English immigrant
craftsman, Thomas Wightman, who is mentioned on
the same receipt. Thomas Seymour and his partner
James Cogswell brought together their best resources
to make this outstanding example of American Neoclassical furniture, and Elizabeth Derby West spared
no expense in obtaining it.

H. 105.4 cm, w. 127 cm, d. 62.2 cm
(H. 41½ in., w. 50 in., d. 24½ in.)
The M. and M. Karolik Collection of Eighteenth-Century
American Arts   23.19

Girandole wall clock
Lemuel Curtis (1790–1857)

Concord, Massachusetts, 1816–21
Carved, painted, and gilt wood; brass; reverse painting on glass

In 1802, Simon Willard of Roxbury, Massachusetts, was granted a patent for the production of "Willard's Patent Time Pieces," an immensely popular wall clock. Lemuel Curtis, like many clockmakers in New England, had links, both familial and professional, with the seminal Willard shop. After completing his apprenticeship, probably with Simon Willard, Curtis opened his own shop in Concord, Massachusetts, in 1811, where he produced timepieces until he departed for Vermont in 1821. Memoirist Edward Jarvis, in his early reminiscences of Concord, recalled that Curtis's shop was "thirty feet long and ten or twelve feet wide. In a room on the left side he repaired and had a small jewelry store. The rest he used by himself, his men and apprentices as a manufactory of his timepieces."

The Museum's girandole wall clock (named for its use of convex glass in the base section) is a type patented by Curtis in 1816 in his attempt to make a more technologically advanced and aesthetically pleasing model that would surpass the influential Willard version. This example is exceptional for its beautifully rendered image of *Marriage* depicted in reverse painting on glass (*eglomisé*), an extraordinarily difficult technique. Curtis asserted in a *Boston Intelligencer* advertisement from April 12, 1817, "Upon the exterior [of his clocks] the exertions of genius and taste have not been spared, or any expence," adding that they received "the approbation of the first artists in the United States" and that they were "the best moddeled, and proportioned, and surpassing, in elegance of appearance, any timepiece ever invented." Other subjects depicted on his clocks include *Commerce* and victorious naval engagements from the War of 1812, fitting themes for "Meeting Houses, Banks, Parlours and other rooms."

H. 116.8 cm, w. 34.9 cm, d. 14.6 cm (H. 46 in., w. 13¾ in., d. 5¾ in.)
Gift of Mrs. Charles C. Cabot in memory of Dr. and Mrs. Charles J. White 1991.241

Bishop mug

Thomas Cains (1779–1865)

South Boston, Massachusetts, about 1821–25
Colorless free-blown flint glass, applied decoration,
silver coin

Thomas Cains, the son of a Gloucestershire glass-
blower, was apprenticed at the Phoenix Glassworks of
Wadham, Ricketts, and Company in Bristol, England.
As part of an initiative to attract skilled glassmakers
to the United States, he was secretly recruited by
Charles F. Kupfer, an agent of the Boston Glass Manufactory. Cains arrived in Boston in April 1812, just
before the beginning of the War of 1812. After the
war's end in 1815, Cains utilized his expertise to produce a full line of table glassware at the South Boston
Flint Glass Works. Later, he established a new enterprise, eventually called the Phoenix Glass Works, perhaps after his old company in England, and this mug
may have been made there in the early 1820s.

This large footed mug is embellished with applied
bands of chain decoration—generally regarded as a
characteristic of Cains's glass—around the widest
section of the lower body. An 1821 American silver
quarter dollar is housed within its hollow stem, an
unusual feature strongly associated with Cains's
work. The mug and another piece of glass descended
directly in the family of Thomas Cains to his great-
great-grandson, whose children gave them to the MFA
in honor of their father. This important history ele-
vates the mug into a virtual Rosetta stone for identi-
fying other pieces of Cains's chain-decorated glass.
Always known in the family as the "Bishop's Mug," the
vessel—possibly a presentation piece—was probably
used to serve a beverage known as bishop, a mulled
port wine flavored with roasted oranges and cloves.

H. 23.8 cm, w. 21.3 cm (H. 9⅜ in., 8⅜ in.)
Gift of William, Nancy and Malcolm in Loving memory of their
father William L. Johnston, Great-Great-Grandson of Thomas
Cains 1995.765

fig. 21. United States silver quarter dollar
(obverse and reverse), designed by John
Reich (1768–1833); engraved by Reich and
Robert Scot (died 1823); minted at
Philadelphia, Pennsylvania, 1818.

Square pier table with canted corners

New York, New York, 1815–20
Rosewood veneer, mahogany veneer,
mahogany, white pine, yellow poplar,
marble

In the second decade of the nineteenth
century, New York City cabinetmakers
produced a variety of sculptural furniture
featuring three-dimensional winged caryatids,
swans, eagles, dolphins, and, as seen here, mythological griffins (or gryphons). Charles-Honoré Lannuier,
Duncan Phyfe, and the firm of Barzilla Deming and
Erastus Bulkley were among the leading producers of
these classical forms derived from English and
French design books issued by Thomas Hope, George
Smith, Charles Percier and Pierre-François-Lèonard
Fontaine, Pierre de la Mésangère, and others.

This pier table (one of a pair) is part of a group of
griffin furniture produced by an as-yet-unidentified
shop. Often associated in the past with Lannuier,
more recent scholarship has tentatively suggested
that the group might have come from Phyfe's shop.
Careful conservation of this table revealed the original burnished gold leaf on the eagle heads and the
green paint (*antique vert*) on the lion bodies. The
gold-leaf ornamental detail around the table's top is
typical of New York workmanship and represents a
less expensive alternative to imported French ormolu
(gilded brass or bronze) mounts.

Griffins (called by Aeschylus "the hounds of Zeus,
who never bark, with beaks like birds") combine the
head and wings of an eagle with the body of a lion.
The example on this table is similar to one depicted in
plate 5 (part D) in *The New-York Book of Prices for
Manufacturing Cabinet and Chair Work,* published
in 1817. Such carved figures were an expensive option
for this type of stylish furniture.

H. 85.7 cm, w. 106 cm, d. 62.9 cm
(H. 33¾ in., w. 41¾ in., d. 24¾ in.)
Museum purchase with funds donated by the W. N. Banks
Foundation   1975.274

Grecian couch

Attributed to Hugh Finlay (1781–1831)

Baltimore, Maryland, about 1820
Yellow poplar, cherry, white pine; rosewood graining
and gilded painting; partial original foundation and new
foundation materials, cover, and trim

The brothers John and Hugh Finlay first advertised their wares in the Baltimore *Federal Gazette* of January 25, 1803. For nearly the next four decades, sometimes working together and sometimes singly, they provided the citizens of that growing and thriving city with such high-style painted furniture as this Grecian couch. At one time, their shop employed as many as sixty-eight craftsmen, including thirty men, thirteen boys, and twenty-five women. They remained current with the changing modes of Neoclassicism; Hugh Finlay, to whom this couch is attributed, even traveled for several months of 1810 in Europe, where he acquired "a number of Drawings, from furniture in the first houses in Paris and London" that he shipped back to his Baltimore shop to use as sources of inspiration for customers seeking "the most approved articles" of furniture.

The couch demonstrates both a sure-handed feel for design, evident in the bold curves and scrolls used to create its outline, and a high quality of painted ornament that enriches the grained wooden surfaces of the front rail and legs. The leafy rosette with an elongated

anthemion seen on the front rail is a signature feature of Finlay's work at this time. Elaborate brass casters, originally tinted with varnish to accentuate their resemblance to gilding, complete the effect.

Perhaps the most compelling visual aspect of this couch, however, is its red silk damask upholstery. Although the couch retains much of its upholstery foundation, its original show cover did not survive. The current cover is a reproduction, based on the surviving threads of the original material trapped under nail heads, while the details and arrangement of a pillow, bolster, and trimming are derived from period prints and other documentation.

H. 90.8 cm, w. 232.4 cm, d. 61.6 cm
(H. 35¾ in., w. 91½ in., d. 24¼ in.)
Gift of Mr. and Mrs. Amos B. Hostetter, Jr., Anne and Joseph P. Pellegrino, Mr. and Mrs. Peter S. Lynch, Mr. William N. Banks, Jr., Eddy G. Nicholson, Mr. and Mrs. John Lastavica, Mr. and Mrs. Daniel F. Morley, and Mary S. and Edward J. Holmes Fund 1988.530

Desk and bookcase

Anthony G. Quervelle (1789–1856)

Philadelphia, Pennsylvania, about 1830

Mahogany, bird's-eye maple, burl ash, yellow poplar, white pine, cedar, maple, glass, pressed glass

Born and trained as a cabinetmaker in France, Anthony Quervelle was in Philadelphia by 1817. He quickly became one of the most important and prolific Philadelphia craftsmen working in the late Neoclassical style, boasting in one advertisement to have "the largest and most fashionable assortment of furniture ever yet offered for sale in this city." The craftsman enhanced his reputation by winning recognition at several mechanical arts competitions, including the Franklin Institute's exhibition in 1827 where he was awarded a silver medal for a closely related desk and bookcase.

Quervelle merged French motifs learned during his early training, probably in Napoleon's imperial workshops, with British forms that were popular in his adopted city. In this majestic desk and bookcase he combines the massive, architectonic form and richly grained woods derived from British designs, with tapered columns, anthropomorphic paw feet, and radiating fan doors that add a French flair. The rounded, inlaid rays of the fan doors made of exquisite mahogany and bird's-eye maple are particularly noteworthy for their technical achievement, as are the carved, veneered, and gilded elements that lavishly ornament the piece. Quervelle also demonstrated his sure grasp of the latest styles by using newly fashionable Gothic arches on the glass doors and interior desk pigeonholes, and pressed glass knobs on the interior drawers.

H. 259.7 cm, w. 125.1 cm, d. 60.9 cm
(H. 102¼ in., w. 49¼ in., d. 24 in.)
Henry H. and Zoe Oliver Sherman Fund   2004.562

Orpheus and Cerberus

Thomas Crawford (1813–1857)
Rome, Italy, 1843
Marble

After studying with the world-renowned Danish sculptor Bertel Thorwaldsen, Thomas Crawford modeled his first major sculpture, *Orpheus and Cerberus,* in clay and plaster while in Rome in 1839. Its subject came from the tenth book of Ovid's *Metamorphoses,* in which Orpheus lulls to sleep the three-headed hellhound Cerberus by playing the lyre, and then rushes past the beast through the gates of Hades in search of his wife Eurydice. For the figure of Orpheus, Crawford was inspired by what was long believed to be the most important masterpiece of antique sculpture, the Apollo Belvedere in the Vatican. Many Americans were introduced to this type of classical sculpture through *Orpheus and Cerberus.*

George Washington Greene, American consul in Rome, and Senator Charles Sumner of Massachusetts were among the admirers of Crawford's work. Sumner successfully encouraged Bostonians to pay by subscription for a marble version of the sculpture, which Crawford completed by 1843. Boston's *Orpheus and Cerberus,* in pristine Seravezza marble, was first exhibited at the Boston Athenaeum, where it was enthusiastically received and helped launch Crawford's career. It remained there until 1872, when it went on "permanent loan" to the Museum of Fine Arts. It was installed at the entrance of the new Museum building, which opened its doors in Copley Square in 1876. *Orpheus and Cerberus* became part of the Museum's collection in 1975, as the gift, fittingly, of Cornelius and Emily Vermeule, scholars of classical art who recognized the work's seminal importance in the history of nineteenth-century American sculpture.

H. 171.5 cm, w. 91.4 cm, d. 137.2 cm
(H. 67½ in., w. 36 in., d. 54 in.)
Gift of Mr. and Mrs. Cornelius Vermeule III 1975.800

Presentation ewer

Baldwin Gardiner (1791–1869)

New York, New York, 1833

Silver

In gratitude for being safely delivered from New Orleans to New York, the passengers of the packet ship *Natchez* presented this silver ewer to Captain Hartwell Reed on July 4, 1833, "As a Testimonial of their estimation of his personal character and seaman-like abilities." The ewer bears the mark of Baldwin Gardiner, the keeper of a fashionable furnishings warehouse at 149 Broadway in New York and brother of Sidney Gardiner of the well-known Philadelphia silversmithing firm Fletcher and Gardiner. Modeled after a classical form, richly decorated and finely crafted, the pitcher is an outstanding example of American silver of the late Neoclassical period. Most of the ornament is repoussé, a labor-intensive technique of hammering the silver from the reverse side to raise the design in relief. Only the border around the lip and the central band are die-rolled, a less expensive machine process used to impress patterns into strips of silver that were then soldered into place. Gardiner's silver manufactory was equipped with the latest technology, including high-pressure steam power, yet he must also have employed craftsmen with the creative abilities and handwork skills required to produce a presentation piece of this caliber.

H. 45 cm, w. 33 cm, diam. base 14.9 cm, wt. 1965.8 gm (H. 17¹¹/₁₆ in., w. 13 in., diam. base 5⅞ in., wt. 63 oz. 4 dwt. 1 gr.)
Gift in honor of Jonathan Fairbanks on the occasion of the silver anniversary of the Department of American Decorative Arts and Sculpture by his many friends and supporters   1996.240

Castor and Pollux

Horatio Greenough (1805–1852)

Florence, Italy, about 1847

Marble

Born in Boston and educated at Harvard, Horatio Greenough showed promise as a sculptor from an early age. With the encouragement of his family and several influential Bostonians, he traveled to Rome in 1825 and became the first American sculptor to pursue training in Italy. Greenough eventually settled in Florence, where he worked with Lorenzo Bartolini, the renowned professor of sculpture at the Accademia di Belle Arti. Bartolini emphasized the study of anatomy, encouraging his students to observe dissections of human cadavers and sketch from live models.

Greenough sculpted a number of important portrait busts, but his most significant commission, received when he was just twenty-seven years old, was a huge marble sculpture of George Washington for the United States Congress, which he modeled on Phidias's Olympian Zeus. The monumental work arrived in the United States in 1841 to mixed reviews. Although most educated people were at least familiar with classical subjects, the subtle classical allusions and partial nudity of Greenough's *Washington* did not win over the American public.

In *Castor and Pollux,* Greenough depicted the brothers in a sophisticated composition within an elliptical boundary, crisply carving the idealized human and equine forms in low relief with a smooth, satiny finish. According to one version of the myth, when Castor was killed in combat, Zeus soothed his grieving twin Pollux by allowing the brothers to spend alternate days among the gods and on earth so they would see each other briefly in passing. In another version, Zeus united them in the sky as the constellation of the twins, or the morning and evening stars. Greenough borrowed elements of both stories, showing the brothers as they cross paths bound for their respective destinations. The stars on their helmets, crescent moon, and clouds place them in the celestial realm.

H. 87.9 cm, w. 114.8 cm, d. 4.4 cm
(H. 34⅝ in., w. 45³/₁₆ in., d. 1¾ in.)
Bequest of Mrs. Horatio Greenough   92.2642

4

American Diversity: Folk Traditions and Vernacular
Expressions Gerald W. R. Ward

The works of art discussed in this chapter largely stand outside the high-style canon and stylistic parameters that characterize the other sections of this book. They also span a wide time period ranging from about 1800 to the present. Although only a small number are included here, they represent a vast body of rich and diverse material that defies easy categorization.

Often, many objects made outside of the so-called mainstream have come to be called *folk art,* narrowly understood as works of art produced in closely knit communities that share a common language, background, and desire to preserve those traditions in the face of outside influences. For example, aside from the English, the largest immigrant group in eighteenth-century North America consisted of Germans, who settled largely in Pennsylvania and North Carolina. Although some of their artistic techniques and decorative motifs permeated mainstream society, the Germanic communities held tightly to their native artistic styles and ways, rebuffing many influences from other sources. Often their works, such as the pie plate attributed to John Neis of Montgomery County, Pennsylvania, feature German text and German-style imagery, such as the tulips here, and thus fall within the classic academic definition of folk art (fig. 22). Similarly, the Vincennes buffet, made by a Montreal-trained cabinetmaker in a French provincial mode on the American frontier, dramatically illustrates the tenacious retentive strength of another European tradition in a different region (p. 120.).

Such ethnic diversity and regional variety are among the great strengths of the Americas. The United States, in poet Walt Whitman's phrase, "is not merely a nation but a teeming Nation of nations," and this rich cultural multiplicity is also evident in Canada, Central America, and South America. Since the initial colo-

fig. 22. Redware plate, attributed to John Neis (1785–1867), Upper Salford Township, Montgomery County, Pennsylvania, 1834.

nization of the continents, immigrant artisans have created works of art influ-enced to greater or lesser degrees by their African, Dutch, English, French, German, Scandinavian, Spanish, or other foreign heritages. They have brought these various countries' artistic and craft traditions to the New World, including preferences for forms, carved ornament, painted decoration, and construction techniques. This process of cultural diffusion and assimilation has continued and remains in effect today.

fig. 23. **Mariner's compass bed quilt, New England,** 1840–50.

The term *folk art*, however, is also used loosely and confusingly to describe an enormous body of material that is perhaps better described by other names, such as vernacular, country, popular, or commercial arts (to list only a few of the possible types), or by names used in the period. For example, recent scholarship has identified and defined a body of exuberant and wildly decorated objects made in the early nineteenth century and known then as "Fancy goods," a middle-class style seen here in a colorful New England bed quilt featuring a dazzling mariner's compass motif (fig. 23).

Indeed, colorful furniture, decorated pottery, weather vanes, decoys, baskets, wood carvings, carousel animals, quilts, bed coverings, and other objects illustrate our inherent desire to beautify utilitarian, even industrial, products, often in idiosyncratic and eclectic ways. In the realm of high-style goods, objects are usually fashioned with a degree of technical proficiency and high-quality materials. While this is also true of many objects outside the mainstream, occasionally in the wider world of popular and vernacular arts, expedient (or even amateurish) craftsmanship and inexpensive materials can result in an expressive, beautiful object. Various mechanized means of production—as with nineteenth-century pressed glass (an American innovation) or silver-plated wares—also can create objects of high visual quality for the average home.

Some of the most compelling objects fashioned in the Americas are those that embody a melding of traditions to create hybrid styles. The large wardrobe attributed to Heinrich Kuenemann and produced in west Texas in the late nineteenth century is a strong example of this synthesis, with its blending of Germanic form, mass-produced imported elements, and local materials (p. 125). Separating and assessing the strands of tradition and innovation that combine to form an American object is often, in the end, what provides a definition of the "American-ness" of American art.

A focus on classification and taxonomy tends to create boundaries between objects and, often, to elevate the products of one's own culture over that of "others." In the end, however, it is the meaning of the object within a given society, its visual quality, and ultimately its affective presence and ability to move the human spirit that are the important qualities of a work of art, be it urban or rural, high style or vernacular, fine or folk.

Buffet

**Attributed to Pierre Antoine Petit, called La Lumière
(died about 1815)**

Vincennes, Indiana, about 1800
Yellow poplar, curly maple, sycamore

By the late seventeenth century, French explorers had traversed what would become the state of Indiana, and by the end of the eighteenth century, French fur-trading posts and small settlements dotted the landscape of the Mississippi River's upper valley, a large territory known as the Illinois Country. Vincennes was the principal settlement in the area. Its population of more than four hundred residents lived a surprisingly refined style of life that included silver spoons, jewelry, and silk clothing. Settled largely by immigrants from French Canada, Vincennes retained a distinctly French character in its architecture and material culture into the early nineteenth century.

This buffet is strongly reminiscent of French provincial furniture made in Normandy and elsewhere at a much earlier date. Its sturdy construction

and decorative detail, including the form of the paneled doors, the carved sunburst ornament in the center of the skirt, and the shape of the curved skirt and feet, clearly align it with the style of Louis XV. It is fashioned, however, from local woods and retains its original finish of red ocher (iron oxide) paint enriched with streaks of a darker pigment.

The buffet may have been made by Pierre Antoine Petit, called La Lumière. A native of Quebec, La Lumière probably trained as a woodworker before heading west to the Illinois Country in the late eighteenth century as an indentured servant. He died there in 1815, "hacked to death" by Potawatomi Indians, according to tradition. Only this buffet and an armoire are currently attributed to his workshop. Later inscriptions on the buffet indicate that it was owned at Saint Mary's of the Woods, a convent established in 1828 in nearby Terre Haute, where two of La Lumière's daughters were enrolled.

H. 117.5 cm, w. 121.9 cm, d. 61.6 cm
(H. 46¼ in., w. 48 in., d. 24¼ in.)
Gift of Daniel and Jessie Lie Farber and
Frank Bemis Fund   1989.50

Pot

J. and E. Norton Pottery (active 1850–1859);
probably decorated by John Hilfinger (1826–1888)
Bennington, Vermont, about 1855–59
Stoneware with cobalt blue decoration

For more than a hundred years, beginning in the late eighteenth century, the potteries of Bennington, Vermont, produced substantial quantities of utilitarian ceramics in various forms. The Norton Pottery, founded by cousins Julius and Edward Norton, made this stoneware pot for the storage of foodstuffs in the late 1850s. It is stamped with their factory mark and the number 4, indicating its capacity in gallons. Edward Norton was a persuasive salesman, and Norton wares were retailed through stores in Vermont, New Hampshire, Massachusetts, and New York, and even as far afield as Galveston, Texas.

Improvements in pottery making enabled the Norton Pottery to make cylindrical (in addition to ovoid) forms by 1850. This advancement, involving the use of revolving molds called "jiggers" and "jollies" that allowed for the turning of circular vessels, may have stimulated a concomitant change in decoration, as the flatter surfaces of the resulting objects were easier to embellish. Alternatively, the desire for more richly ornamented objects—perhaps needed to catch the eye in an increasingly competitive marketplace—may have led to the technological developments. Whatever the relationship, the result was an efflorescence of painted Bennington pottery in the 1850s.

The itinerant artist John Hilfinger may have painted the cobalt blue images on this pot, rendering a spotted standing stag and resting doe amid fences and foliage. Born in Württemberg, Germany, Hilfinger came to America in the mid-nineteenth century, and during his career he decorated ceramics from Massachusetts, Vermont, and New York potteries in his characteristic exuberant manner. As a blend of Yankee technology and immigrant artistry, the Norton pot is an outstanding expression of a common melding of influences in American decorative arts.

H. 30.5 cm, diam. 33 cm (H. 12 in., diam. 13 in.)
Gift of Mrs. Lloyd E. Hawes in memory of Nina Fletcher Little
1993.546

Storage jar

Dave Drake (or Dave the Potter; about 1800–about 1870) for Lewis J. Miles Pottery
Edgefield District, South Carolina, 1857
Stoneware with alkaline glaze

The Edgefield District of South Carolina, noted for its fine and abundant clays, is one of the South's leading pottery-making areas. In the years before the Civil War, many of the workers in the area's potteries were enslaved black men and women. One of these slaves, known for most of his life simply as "Dave the Potter," was a skilled craftsman who produced aesthetically pleasing and technically accomplished stoneware vessels between about 1830 and 1864. That part of Dave's story is not necessarily unusual; what *is* unusual is that Dave was literate and, for whatever reason, his owners allowed him to sign his work. This vessel, for example, is signed "Dave" on each side and dated "Aug. 22, 1857," a day right in the middle of Dave's peak production.

Moreover, about 25 percent of Dave's surviving pots are inscribed with verses—sometimes biblical, often humorous, ironic, or poignant—that reveal his keen intelligence and his facility with language. This capacious example bears the rhymed couplet: "I made this Jar for Cash- / though its called lucre trash." Dave also added the initials "Lm" for his owner at the time, Lewis Miles, and other inscriptions.

During his life, Dave was bought and sold several times. After emancipation, he adopted the surname of one of his early owners, Drake. Dave apparently passed away between 1870 and 1880, leaving behind an important legacy of vessels that are testimony to his skill and personality and to the ability of the human spirit to express itself even under the most difficult conditions.

H. 48.3 cm, diam. 45.1 cm (H. 19 in., diam. 17¾ in.)
Harriet Otis Cruft Fund and Otis Norcross Fund   1997.10

Peacock weather vane

Eastern United States, about 1860–75
Copper, painted gold; iron

Perched delicately on a round ball, this striking peacock weather vane formed a strong sculptural silhouette against the sky. Its head, featuring a pierced eye
and pointed beak, is topped by a stylized tripartite
comb. The long curving neck descends gracefully to
the body, where the thin legs and talons grasp the ball
support. The flat, ribbed tail provides a wide expanse
of metal that would effectively catch the wind, and
the hollow body, made of molded copper sheets soldered together, is painted gold to protect the vane
from the elements. Although such details would
hardly have been visible from ground level, the arti-
san delicately applied paint to the body and the tail in
imitation of feathers. The iron rod originally would
have also supported iron letters indicating the cardi-
nal points of north, south, east, and west.

In a world in which changes in wind speed and
direction were often the best indicators of a coming
storm, weather vanes served a useful as well as
ornamental purpose. They were a common sight
in the early United States, mounted atop churches,
civic buildings, and domestic residences. Although
they could be fashioned in almost any form, many
weather vanes depicted creatures of the natural
world, including codfish, horses, goats, sheep, cows,
and grasshoppers. The maker of this weather vane
is not known, but the influential New York dealer of
folk and modern art Edith Halpert found it and two
related examples in Vermont sometime between
1929 and 1953.

H. 50.2 cm, w. 85.8 cm, d. 10.2 cm
(H. 19¾ in., w. 35¾ in., d. 4 in.)
Gift of Maxim Karolik   54.1089

Greyhound carousel figure

Charles I. D. Looff (1852–1918)

Riverside, Rhode Island, about 1905–10

Painted wood, glass

During the heyday of the carousel (or merry-go-round) as a popular form of American entertainment, from the 1890s into at least the 1920s, as many as three thousand carousels were installed at amusement parks across the country. Many of the finest carvers of carousel animals were German immigrants, including Charles Looff, whose name is stamped on the belly of this colorful, imposing greyhound.

Looff was born in Schleswig-Holstein on the border between Denmark and Germany and moved to New York in 1870 as a young man of eighteen. He found employment first as a furniture carver, and, according to tradition, carved carousel figures in the evenings as a hobby. Within five years, he opened his first carousel at Coney Island, and in 1880 he established a carousel factory in Brooklyn. The plant remained in operation there until Looff shifted his headquarters to the Crescent Park Hippodrome in Riverside, Rhode Island, about 1904–5. This greyhound is marked "Riverside" and was thus made there between 1905 and 1910, when Looff moved his factory to California.

Looff's factories produced an extensive menagerie of animals, including a small number of greyhounds—perhaps only a dozen—all said to be modeled on a family pet. This example is a large "stander," used on the outer ring of the carousel. Its "romance" side (the side exposed to the outside as the carousel rotates counterclockwise) is richly embellished with carved details, applied tassels, and cut-glass decoration. When acquired by the Museum, the greyhound was painted dark brown and covered with a thick layer of varnish. A painstaking process of conservation removed about fourteen layers of paint (carousel figures were exposed to the weather and thus repainted frequently), revealing the original polychrome painted surface and other details.

H. 137.2 cm, w. 185.4 cm, d. 38.1 cm
(H. 54 in., w. 73 in., d. 15 in.)
Gift of Claire M. and Robert
N. Ganz   1992.267

Wardrobe

Heinrich Kuenemann II (1843–1914)

Fredericksburg, Texas, about 1870
Southern yellow pine

By the 1840s, a wave of German immigration had spread to the Hill Country of Texas, virtually on the border of Comanche territory. The population of some towns, including Fredericksburg in Gillespie County, was about 85 percent German in the 1860s. Like English joiners in seventeenth-century New England, many Texas German woodworkers initially attempted to replicate the conditions of their mother country, producing furniture in the Biedermier style (popular in Germany and Austria, and to a lesser extent elsewhere, from the 1820s to the 1840s, featuring simple, clean lines, restrained ornament, and, often, light-colored woods such as maple). Soon, however, societal influences — among them migration and improved postal and communication systems — led to changes in the materials and design of their work.

Heinrich Kuenemann, one of at least ten woodworkers in Fredericksburg, was born in Steterdorf, Hanover, Germany, and arrived in Galveston, Texas, in 1845 as a two-year-old. He married Dorothea Elisabeth Tatsch on January 3, 1869, thus becoming the son-in-law of Johann Peter Tatsch, a well-known Prussian-born woodworker with whom Kuenemann may have served his apprenticeship. Tatsch gave the newlyweds a large wardrobe that surely inspired Kuenemann when he fashioned this example.

Kuenemann's imposing joined wardrobe, or *Kleiderschrank,* is an architectonic type of bedroom storage furniture favored by continental Europeans. Although the piece is Germanic in form, its mass-produced ornament, including the roundel in the cornice, the drawer pulls, and the applied rope-turned spindles at the sides, is evocative of the Renaissance and Elizabethan revival furniture made in Midwestern factories and imported into Texas at the time. Its creation from southern yellow pine, however, immediately identifies the wardrobe as a distinctly local product. The dramatic curly pine panels selected for the doors and drawer fronts present a dazzling optical effect, reminiscent of Baroque furniture made some two centuries earlier. This complex blend of attributes reflects, in three-dimensional form, the social and cultural factors that characterized life in the Hill Country in the 1870s.

H. 221.7 cm, w. 143.5 cm, d. 59.7 cm
(H. 87¼ in., w. 56½ in., d. 23½ in.)
Gift of Mrs. Charles L. Bybee   1990.483

San Ysidro Labradór

Raymond López (b. 1961)

Santa Fe, New Mexico, about 2000

Painted and carved wood

Santos (devotional images of saints made for Catholic churches and homes) are one of the oldest living traditions in Hispanic American art. They have been fashioned in three principal forms: *bultos* (painted wood sculptures, as here), *retablos* (painted wood panels), and *ex-votos* (painted images on tin-plated sheets of iron). Examples were imported into New Mexico from Spain and Mexico before 1600, and by the eighteenth century *bultos* **and** *retablos* were also produced there by local *santeros,* who developed a distinctive New Mexican style. That tradition has been maintained into the twenty-first century by a vibrant community of New Mexico artists that continues to create not only colorful *santos,* but furniture, textiles, paintings, tinwork, straw appliqué, and other objects in the Spanish colonial mode as well.

This image of the patron saint of farmers, San Ysidro Labradór (or Saint Isidore the Farmer, or the Laborer), was carved by furniture maker and *santero* Raymond López of Santa Fe. His work was first exhibited in 1993 at Spanish Market, a longstanding annual festival held in Santa Fe and sponsored by the Spanish Colonial Arts Society. A number of stories and legends concern Ysidro, a Spanish farmer who died in 1130. In one, as depicted here, an angel is helping him with his plowing. In another story, he is said to have caused a fountain of fresh water to spring from the ground to assuage his master's thirst. Such a miraculous talent made San Ysidro a particularly meaningful image to residents of perpetually arid New Mexico.

H. 43.2 cm, w. 29.2 cm, d. 57.2 cm
(H. 17 in., w. 11½ in., d. 22½ in.)
Promised gift of James and Margie Krebs

5

Revivalism and Eclecticism: The Mid- and Late Nineteenth Century

Kelly H. L'Ecuyer

Between the early nineteenth century and the outbreak of World War I, the United States transformed itself from a fledgling nation into a world leader controlling vast territories and natural resources from the Atlantic coast to the Pacific and holding commensurate international political and economic power. Aiding this transformation was the Industrial Revolution, which had begun in the late eighteenth century and was realized in the first half of the nineteenth. Industrialization created a new middle class (along with growing disparities between the richest and poorest Americans), helped concentrate population in urban centers, and shifted production of many material goods away from small, artisan-owned shops to large-scale manufactories employing dozens or even hundreds of workers. Advances in communications (inexpensive newspapers, books, and periodicals) and transportation (canals, steamboats, and railroads) allowed greater dissemination not only of ideas about design and style, but also raw materials and finished products.

In this environment of rapid social and economic change, American artists and craftsmen drew upon a barrage of artistic influences from abroad. Linking the diverse array of stylistic influences was a romantic and picturesque aesthetic that had emerged in Europe in the late eighteenth century. Romanticism, as it is often called, spurred a general interest in mining past cultures for design ideas that carried aesthetically and emotionally appealing associations. Romanticism emphasized viewers' subjective responses to landscapes, architecture, and works of art that were charged with emotion, dramatized with irregularities and contrasts, and enriched with the patina of age. It thus offered a contrast to the cool rationalism of the Neoclassical taste.

Romantic sensibilities were most prominent among American artists at midcentury, when, like their counterparts abroad, they freely selected and combined elements of numerous revival styles in modern forms, striving to capture the

fig. 24. Souvenir kerchief from Philadelphia Centennial Exhibition, probably Philadelphia, Pennsylvania, about 1876.

spirit and associations of the past rather than creating direct imitations. Ongoing archaeological investigations at ancient sites in Egypt, Italy, and Greece, and numerous publications illustrating historical architecture, furnishing, and ornament inspired eclectic design in the decorative arts. Choosing from a broad menu of styles, American artists and designers produced creative and overlapping interpretations of Egyptian, Grecian, Gothic, Roman, Italianate, Renaissance, Elizabethan, and French courtly styles. French styles in particular came to represent the height of fashion, and the Rococo Revival, an exuberant interpretation of the eighteenth-century French Rococo style, was popular for decades. Rococo Revival elements, including undulating scrolls, lush floral motifs, and bold, asymmetrical ornament, appeared in both high-end and middle-range decorative arts objects.

Throughout the nineteenth century, American consumers and artisans alike learned about the latest European styles and craft practices through contact with skilled immigrants, grand international exhibitions, and widely available publications. Highly trained immigrant craftsmen, many of whom were displaced by numerous European political upheavals beginning in the 1840s and 1850s, were eagerly recruited by American manufacturing firms and small shops to create high-end work using specialized craft techniques. Spectacular international exhibitions, such as the Great Exhibition of 1851 in London's Crystal Palace and the Philadelphia Centennial Exhibition of 1876 (fig. 24), also introduced millions to industrial and artistic products from around the world. Included were displays by the United States and participating European nations, as well as by cultures of the Near East and Asia. As early as the 1840s, widely circulated pattern books and periodicals like *Godey's Lady's Book* made new styles available to people living in rural areas and the ever-expanding western territories.

While American craftsmen readily adapted new styles and techniques in the decorative arts, many American-born sculptors found few opportunities for training and work in the United States. Instead, they traveled to Europe, particularly Rome, for study and inspiration. Whereas the first generation of American sculptors to study and travel abroad, including Horatio Greenough, Hiram Powers, and Thomas Crawford in the early nineteenth century, had produced work closely modeled on ancient Greek and Roman examples, the second generation, working in the mid-nineteenth century, created sculpture that was more freely adapted from classical sources. Influenced by midcentury Romanticism, the work of second-generation artists Harriet Hosmer, William Rimmer, William Wetmore Story, and others incorporated emotional nuance, literary symbolism, and psychological drama. In the late nineteenth century, the center for studying sculpture shifted from Rome to Paris, and a third generation of sculptors, including Augustus Saint-Gaudens and Daniel Chester French, were influenced by the Ecole des Beaux-Arts and other Parisian schools. Rather than taking inspiration from the smooth marble sculptures of Greek and Roman classicism, these artists looked to Renaissance sources and developed lively and expressive works in bronze.

In the United States, the Civil War hindered the production of decorative arts objects for a time in the 1860s, as it disrupted trade and diverted many raw materials to military purposes and largely prevented consumers from accumulating enough wealth to adopt significant new styles. Beginning in the 1870s, postwar economic recovery and flourishing industrial and commercial development led to the creation of newly monied families and a thriving middle class in northern states and expanding western territories. These prosperous consumers provided a ready market for up-to-date furnishings in the lavishly ornamented styles of the Aesthetic Movement and the American Renaissance.

fig. 25. **Enrico Meneghelli** (1853–after 1912), *The Picture Gallery at the Old Museum,* Boston, Massachusetts, 1879.

The Aesthetic Movement of the 1870s and 1880s was the first of many design reform efforts in the late nineteenth and early twentieth centuries to come about as a response to the florid and often heavy-looking revival styles that dominated the decorative arts of the 1840s through the 1860s. Proponents of the movement sought to create interiors that artfully juxtaposed objects from many cultures and styles, using delicate harmonies of color, texture, and pattern to create aesthetically pleasing compositions. The natural motifs, abstract patterns, and asymmetry found in the arts of Japan and the Near East became essential sources for Aesthetic designs, which placed a new emphasis on rich two-dimensional patterning of flat surfaces, particularly through intricate wallpapers, fabrics, and inlaid, ebonized, and gilt furniture. Millionaire industrialists hired firms such as Herter Brothers to create brilliantly unified Aesthetic interiors, while popular magazines and books encouraged middle-class homeowners to create "artistic" interiors with busily patterned wallpapers and collections of exotic bric-a-brac. The new emphasis on collecting, display, and connoisseurship coincided with the formation of the country's first comprehensive public museums, including the Museum of Fine Arts, Boston, which was incorporated in 1870 (fig. 25).

At the end of the century, Americans' new wealth, confidence, and cosmopolitanism were more self-consciously displayed in the American Renaissance movement. While Aesthetic Movement artists focused on domestic interiors, those of the American Renaissance created grand public spaces, stately institutions, and idealistic sculpture, such as Augustus Saint-Gaudens's *Head of Victory*, a small-scale study for a large public commission (p. 149). The art and architecture produced in this vein, unlike earlier revival styles, emphasized the scholarly study and historical accuracy of forms appropriated from Renaissance Italy, France, and England. The use of these courtly styles in public settings implied that the United States was the successor to the great civilizations of the past.

Mechanization and factory production allowed the latest fashions to be translated into products for nearly every consumer's price range, thus democratizing the diffusion of styles. Handcrafted objects such as the lavish chalice and paten by Cooper and Fisher and the factory-made silver-plated caster set by Roswell Gleason and Sons shared Gothic Revival motifs yet differed dramatically in price (pp. 136–37). The demarcation between large-scale production and handcraftsmanship was not always sharp; some firms, such as silversmiths Eoff and Shepard, outfitted their shops with the latest machinery in order to speed production but also used highly refined handwork for elaborate presentation pieces. By the late nineteenth century, handwork persisted only in the most expensive, high-end goods. The prevalence of factory goods made by unskilled workers in assembly-line fashion would lead reformers to call for a renewal of preindustrial values in the Arts and Crafts Movement.

Chalice and paten

Cooper and Fisher (active 1854–1862)

New York, New York, 1855

Silver, silver gilt, enamel

Francis W. Cooper's career as a silversmith spanned nearly fifty years, but he produced his most ambitious pieces between 1854 and 1862, during his partnership with Richard Fisher. This exceptional chalice and paten, the cup and dish used to serve wine and bread in the Christian communion service, represent Cooper and Fisher's finest work in the Gothic Revival style. More broadly, these objects reflect efforts by reformers in the American Episcopal Church to capture the perceived simplicity and purity of the medieval Christian church.

The New York Ecclesiological Society, formed in 1848 and based on an English counterpart, championed liturgical reforms and hoped to re-create a medieval setting for worship through the careful design of churches and religious objects. Acting on behalf of New York's Episcopal churches, the society engaged Francis Cooper as its exclusive silversmith to produce communion silver in what they termed the "correct" Gothic style, based on interpretations of early medieval art and architecture. Cooper and Fisher made this chalice and paten as part of a larger communion service created for the dedication of New York's Trinity Chapel in 1855. Designed by architect Richard Upjohn, Trinity Chapel was built on West 25th Street near Broadway as a satellite of the older Trinity Church located on Wall Street. The communion set was based on similar designs published by contemporary English designers and reformers.

The richly ornamented set is some of the earliest enameled silver hollowware crafted in the United States. The high quality of the work can be attributed to the skills of two specialist craftsmen employed in the Cooper and Fisher shop: Henry P. Horlor, an enamelist, and an engraver known today only by his last name of Segel. These and other artisans in the shop used a wide range of Gothic vocabulary, including pointed arches, quatrefoils, spiral columns, angels, and foliage, consistent with the church's architecture. On the chalice's six-lobed foot, enameled panels depicting biblical scenes alternate with engraved panels illustrating the lives of saints. The paten displays a central enameled panel of Christ in Majesty surrounded by Gothic-style script. Superbly crafted, these objects are among the most ambitious and lavish church silver made in mid-nineteenth-century America.

Chalice: H. 25.1 cm, diam. rim 14 cm, wt. 916.1 gm
(H. 9⅞ in., diam. rim 5½ in., wt. 29 oz. 9 dwt. 2 gr.)
Paten: H. 0.5 cm, diam. 24.2 cm, wt. 445.8 gm
(H. ½ in., diam. 9½ in., wt. 14 oz. 6 dwt. 16 gr.)
Gift of The Seminarians, Curator's Fund, and Ron Bourgeault
1996.27.1–2

Magic Caster

Roswell Gleason and Sons (about 1850–1871)

Dorchester, Massachusetts, about 1857–71

Silver plate, cut glass

Table casters, as these sets were known in the mid-nineteenth century, comprised decorative stands holding cut-glass bottles containing condiments such as salt, pepper, sugar, oil, vinegar, and possibly mustard. Most silver-plate manufacturers produced casters, but the Magic Caster was an especially elaborate novelty product that Roswell Gleason and Sons patented in 1857. With a twist of a knob, its six revolving doors opened all at once to reveal six glass bottles inside. This clever device appealed to the love of new "mechanized" technologies and complicated dining accoutrements by upper- and middle-class consumers of the period. An English acquaintance of Gleason, upon showing a Magic Caster to his family, wrote in 1856 that "the Patent Castor in England would be a very saleable article; the extreme neatness and usefulness, combined with its novelty & elegance, would command much attention." The caster's decorative ornament included pointed arches in the Gothic Revival mode and such dining-related images as pendant swags of dead game animals and fish much like the carving on a contemporary sideboard by Ignatius Lutz (see p. 141).

Born in rural Vermont, Roswell Gleason was a very successful self-made man. After moving to Dorchester, Massachusetts, in his youth, he became a tin worker in 1822 and a pewterer by 1830. He successfully grew his business, employing more than one hundred workers at a large factory and expanding to encompass britannia (tin alloy) wares. After 1850, when his sons joined the company, the firm produced mainly silver-plated goods. Their 1866 catalogue depicts more than sixty varieties of table casters in various sizes, including two versions of the Magic Caster on the first page, along with hundreds of other types of fancy tablewares.

H. 55.9 cm, w. 22.2 cm, d. 22.2 cm (H. 22 in., w. 8¾ in., d. 8¾ in.)
Marion E. Davis Fund   1984.23

Table

Alexander Roux (about 1813–1886)
New York, New York, 1850–57
Rosewood, rosewood veneer

Alexander Roux was one of the elite New York cabinetmakers of French and German descent who supplied high-style furniture in the latest fashions to wealthy patrons in New York and beyond. Having emigrated from France in 1835, Roux quickly established his business, first as an upholsterer and then as a cabinetmaker, alongside other purveyors of luxury goods in the elegant Broadway shopping district. He made furniture in the French styles in vogue during the mid-nineteenth century, emphasizing his French training and ancestry in his advertising. Architect Andrew Jackson Downing singled out Roux's work for praise in his landmark 1850 book *The Architecture of Country Houses,* writing: "At the warehouse of M. A. Roux, Broadway, may be found a large collection of furniture for the drawing-room, library, etc.—the most tasteful designs of Louis Quatorze, Renaissance, Gothic, etc., to be found in the country...."

This elegant table with exquisite carving in high relief displays Roux's free handling of a variety of French styles drawn from Rococo Revival and Renaissance sources. It bears his stenciled label— "From / A. Roux / French / Cabinet Maker / Nos. 479 & 481 Broadway / New York"—advertising not only his business location but also his fashionably French origins.

H. 80 cm, w. 137.2 cm, d. 61.6 cm
(H. 31½ in., w. 54 in., d. 24¼ in.)
Frank B. Bemis Fund   1983.325

Ewer

Eoff and Shepard (active 1852–1860);
retailed by Ball, Black, and Company (1852–1874)
New York, New York, about 1860
Silver

This grand ewer ornamented with elaborate maritime motifs was exhibited by the silver retailers Ball, Black, and Company at New York's 1864 Metropolitan Fair. The fair was one of many held in northern states during the Civil War to benefit medical care and hospitals for Union soldiers through the United States Sanitary Commission. Bostonian John Williams Quincy purchased the ewer at the fair and had it engraved as a memorial to his grandfather, Captain Silas Atkins, following the wishes of Quincy's late mother, Abigail Atkins Quincy. The urn-shaped vessel is awash with nautical images, including the face of Neptune above an angel figurehead; sea nymphs and dolphins amid frothy waves; and three-dimensional anchors, chains, and seashells. A figure of a sailor with a spyglass perched astride the ewer's handle is a fitting tribute to the successful Boston mariner Captain Atkins.

Silversmiths Edgar Mortimer Eoff and George L. Shepard maintained a partnership for nearly a decade. Their midsize silver-manufacturing business, which employed twenty-five men and boys, produced high-quality silver in a modern shop outfitted with six thousand dollars' worth of tools and steam-powered machinery. While they sold some domestic and church silver directly to New York clients, they also supplied prestigious retailers like Ball, Black, and Company. This presentation ewer represents the most elaborate work in their range of production.

H. 49.5 cm, w. 24 cm, diam. base 16.5 cm, wt. 2089.9 gm
(H. 19½ in., w. 9⅜ in., diam. base 6½ in., wt. 67 oz. 3 dwt. 20 gr.)
Helen and Alice Colburn Fund   1977.620

Sideboard

Ignatius Lutz (active 1844–1860)

Philadelphia, Pennsylvania, 1850–60

Oak, yellow poplar, marble

The lavish, naturalistic carving on this massive sideboard—including a stag's head, dead game birds, bulging clusters of fruits, and grotesque animal faces—may be unsettling to viewers today. However, to affluent Americans of the 1850s and 1860s, this imposing object signified the owner's wealth and power, and its emblems of hunt and harvest celebrated abundance and prosperity. The sideboard's fine workmanship and large scale created a dramatic presence in the dining room, where it displayed costly silver objects and set the scene for elaborate dining rituals. In a metaphoric sense, as scholar Kenneth L. Ames has argued, sideboards like this one represented the transformation of hunting and eating into a refined and domesticated experience and thus symbolized for their owners the triumph of human civilization over the natural world.

Sideboards trace their form, function, and iconography to noble homes in Europe, where such pieces had been in use since the fifteenth century. The seminal examples of nineteenth-century sideboards with dining-related carvings originated in France, as did many of the immigrant craftsmen who produced similar works in the United States. Ignatius Lutz was one of several French-trained cabinetmakers who dominated the high-end furniture trade in America, bringing European styles and craftsmanship to a wealthy and fashionable clientele. Lutz's shop, employing thirty craftsmen, was among the largest in Philadelphia and relied upon handwork rather than power machinery to produce masterpieces such as this sideboard.

H. 238.8 cm, w. 188 cm, d. 63.5 cm (H. 94 in., w. 74 in., d. 25 in.)
Gift of the Estate of Richard Bruce E. Lacont 1990.1

Painted bedstead with canopy

Heywood Brothers and Company;
painting traditionally attributed to Thomas Hill
(1829–1908) and Edward Hill (1843–1923)
Gardner, Massachusetts, about 1855
Painted pine

American painted furniture encompasses elegant, high-style objects such as the Thomas Seymour commode painted by John Ritto Penniman (see p. 102–103), vernacular furniture such as Pennsylvania German blanket chests, and a wide range of styles in between. This bedstead is a particularly grand example of the middle-class cottage furniture popularized in the 1850s by illustrations in the widely circulating magazine *Godey's Lady's Book.* Architect and tastemaker Andrew Jackson Downing, in his seminal 1850 publication *The Architecture of Country Houses,* described cottage furniture as "remarkable for its combination of lightness and strength, and its essentially cottage-like character. It is very highly finished . . . Some of the better sets have groups of flowers or other designs painted upon them with artistic skill."

Heywood Brothers made this bedstead for Levi Heywood, the president of the company. It was crafted of inexpensive pine, like other cottage furniture, but its painted decoration—attributed (according to company tradition) to the English-born brothers Thomas and Edward Hill—is exceptionally rich and elaborate. The ebonized surface is ornamented with hand-painted fruit and floral still life arrangements surrounded by Rococo Revival gilt borders. The landscape paintings on the headboard are of particular interest, as the Hill brothers went on to become distinguished painters of the American West and the White Mountains of New Hampshire.

H. 224.8 cm, w. 161.3 cm, d. 214.6 cm
(H. 88½ in., w. 63½ in., d. 84½ in.)
Gift of Richard N. Greenwood 1978.305

Sappho

William Wetmore Story (1819–1895)

Rome, Italy, 1863

Marble

The subject of this sculpture, Sappho of Lesbos, the sixth-century-B.C. Greek poet, was a virtual Rohrschach test for nineteenth-century intellectuals, who often interpreted what little is actually known of her life and work to reflect their own predilections. For example, one journal stated in 1859 that Sappho was of "warm poetic temperament, of great lyric power, of voluptuous, passionate yearnings, and of many moral shortcomings." William Wetmore Story saw her differently and chose to portray her in a calm, ideal pose. Seated in a *klismos* chair, she contemplates throwing herself off a cliff into the sea after her rejection by the Greek ferryman Phaon. A wilting rose, a symbol of failed love, droops across her unstrung lyre, contributing to the mood of listless reverie.

Story was born in Salem, Massachusetts, and raised in Cambridge. He was the son of Joseph Story, a justice of the U.S. Supreme Court and law professor at Harvard University. Although he followed his father into the legal profession, earning a law degree in 1840, his real interests lay in art, music, and literature. After his father's death in 1845, a committee of Cambridge citizens invited him to create a memorial to his father for Mount Auburn Cemetery. Having no experience in making monumental sculpture, Story moved with his family to Rome to study portrait memorials. The monument to his father was completed and accepted in 1853, and Story returned to his law practice in Boston in 1855. The next year, however, he permanently abandoned the legal profession and settled his family in Rome. He began producing idealized sculptures of literary and mythological subjects, but his work received little recognition until his friend Nathaniel Hawthorne used Story's sculpture of Cleopatra as the subject of his novel *The Marble Faun*, published in 1860.

H. 139.4 cm, w. 81.6 cm, d. 86.4 cm (H. 54⅞ in., w. 32⅛ in., d. 34 in.)
Otis Norcross Fund   1977.772

The Sleeping Faun

Harriet Goodhue Hosmer (1830–1908)

Rome, Italy, about 1865

Marble

Exhibited before millions of visitors at international exhibitions, Harriet Hosmer's depiction of an inebriated faun sprawled against a tree stump was one of her most highly acclaimed works. Contemporary critics agreed that Hosmer had captured the graceful curves and sensual finishes of Greek Hellenistic sculpture in the adolescent faun's perfect proportions, smooth skin, and languorous pose, while at the same time evoking a mood of playfulness and whimsy. The bunch of grapes and the panpipe littered on the ground refer to the faun's merry carousing, and his pointed ears and tiger-skin drapery indicate his animalistic nature. In counterpoint to his peaceful sleep, a mischievous satyr ties the faun to the tree stump with the ends of the tiger skin. Hosmer employed tremendous carving skill to create the varied textures of the faun's sensual body, the rough tiger skin, the mossy forest floor, the firm grapes, and the satyr's thick, curly hair.

One of the nineteenth century's most accomplished female artists, Hosmer received a progressive education at a boarding school in Lenox, Massachusetts, where her mentors encouraged her to seek a way of life not bound by then current conventions of womanhood. She began studying sculpture in the United States but moved to Rome in 1852 to advance her education, becoming the first American woman sculptor to do so.

There, she studied with England's leading Neoclassical sculptor, John Gibson. By the mid-1850s Hosmer's work was received warmly by critics, and she became a colorful figure in American and European artistic circles, known for her unorthodox lifestyle. In a testimonial to her own independence, Hosmer remarked in 1868, "I honor every woman who has strength enough to step outside the beaten path when she feels that her walk lies in another; strength enough to stand up and be laughed at, if necessary."

H. 87.6 cm, w. 104.1 cm, d. 41.9 cm
(H. 34½ in., w. 41 in., d. 16½ in.)
Gift of Mrs. Lucien Carr
12.709

Goblet

New England Glass Company (1818–1888);
engraved by Louis Vaupel (1824–1903)

East Cambridge, Massachusetts, about 1860–75
Blown cobalt blue cased glass, cut and engraved

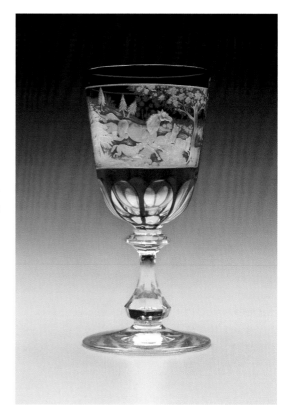

Louis Vaupel's work at the New England Glass Company represents the pinnacle of mid-nineteenth-century glass engraving. He came to the company in 1850 from Germany, where he had learned his craft from his father and had already attained the rank of an expert glass engraver. Vaupel specialized in cased (or overlay) glass, made of fused layers of colored and clear glass into which decoration was cut with a grinding wheel. Artisans had produced glass of this type in Europe, particularly in Bohemia, since the eighteenth century, and displays of glass from France and Austria at New York's Crystal Palace exhibition in 1853 helped popularize the style in America.

Engraving cased glass required great skill and speed. The craftsman would begin by either lightly drawing the design on the surface of the glass or placing a piece of paper showing the design inside the vessel. He then used varying sizes of copper grinding wheels, which were coated with an abrasive agent such as emery or pumice mixed with oil, to engrave the design. As the grinding wheel turned on a lathe, the craftsman delicately pressed the layered glass against the spinning blade, which removed areas of colored glass to reveal the clear glass beneath. Because the abrasive material and glass dust partially obscured the glass, the engraver relied on a sense of touch to judge the amount of pressure needed to create the design. In the complex hunting scenes on this remarkable goblet, Vaupel skillfully created precise renderings of the animals' musculature and a lively sense of movement and depth.

H. 15.9 cm, w. 7.6 cm, d. 7.6 cm (H. 6¼ in., w. 3 in., d. 3 in.)
Bequest of Dr. Minette D. Newman   61.1219

Cabinet

Nelson Gustafson (active 1873–1875)
New York, New York, about 1873–75
Mahogany, rosewood, exotic woods, porcelain
and bronze plaques

During the 1860s and 1870s, fashionable furniture moved away from the sculptural Rococo Revival styles of the 1850s toward a revival of classical elements from various historical sources. The new style drew from the architectural forms of the Renaissance, the French Neoclassical furniture of the eighteenth century, and the French Second Empire. This drawing-room cabinet, stamped in multiple places "N. GUSTAFFSON," has a tripartite shape divided by scrolled pilasters, concave side panels, and a flat pedestal on top intended for displaying a work of art, perhaps a clock or sculpture. It uses a decorative vocabulary seen in other furniture forms of the period, including ebonized elements (painted black to resemble ebony), incised and gilt linear decoration, contrasting exotic woods, marquetry (decorative inlaid wood) panels, and bronze, gilt-bronze, and porcelain plaques.

Although little is known about Nelson Gustafson, who is listed in New York City directories only from 1873 to 1875, he evidently ran a shop producing luxury furniture that required the contributions of many craftsmen. The marquetry panels may have been imported from France. The gilt-bronze mounts are stamped "P.E.G.," for P. E. Guerin, a New York firm founded in 1857 by French-born immigrant Pierre Emmanuel Guerin. Guerin specialized in producing French-style bronze medallions and hardware, and he successfully competed with imported ornamental hardware by offering locally made custom work to New York manufacturers.

H. 143.5 cm, w. 179.1 cm, d. 41.9 cm
(H. 56½ in., w. 70½ in., d. 16½ in.)
Edwin E. Jack Fund 1981.400

Mildred Howells

Augustus Saint-Gaudens (1848–1907); Frame
probably designed by Stanford White (1853–1906)

New York, New York, 1898

Bronze, brown patina, lost-wax cast; wood frame
Diam. relief 53.3 cm (21 in.); h. frame 78.7 cm,
w. frame 73.7 cm (h. frame 31 in., w. frame 29 in.)
Gift of Miss Mildred Howells   57.558

Head of Victory

Augustus Saint-Gaudens (1848–1907)
Probably cast by the Gorham Manufacturing
Company (1865–1961)

Providence, Rhode Island, 1907

Bronze, green-brown patina, lost-wax cast; marble base
H. including base 31.8 cm, w. 19.7, d. 17.1 cm
(H. including base 12½ in., w. 7¾ in., d. 6¾ in.)
Helen and Alice Colburn Fund   1977.600

These two sculptures represent the range of work—
both domestic and public—produced by the leading
sculptor of the American Renaissance period, Augustus Saint-Gaudens. Apprenticed to a New York cameo
cutter, Saint-Gaudens later studied sculpture at the
École des Beaux-Arts in Paris. He collaborated on
important commissions with the famed architects
Henry Hobson Richardson, Charles McKim, and Stanford White and is perhaps best known for his path-
breaking work in bronze.

In his bronze reliefs, which reflect his admiration
for the fine reliefs by Italian Renaissance masters
Pisanello and Donatello, Saint-Gaudens employed
subtle textures and a multitude of painterly effects
that create depth and liveliness of surface. He
excerpted the portrait of Mildred Howells, a celebrated poet and watercolorist, from a double portrait
relief (now lost) of Mildred and her father, the writer
and editor William Dean Howells. Saint-Gaudens,
who admired both father and daughter, proposed the
project himself. Mildred's forthright gaze, elegant
profile, and jaunty pose with her hand on her hip
reveal a stylish and confident young woman. The

relief is set in its original frame, believed to have been
designed by Saint-Gaudens's friend Stanford White.

The *Head of Victory* is one of several studies for
Saint-Gaudens's last great public sculpture, the *Sherman Monument*, commissioned by the State of New
York for the Grand Army Plaza in New York City and
completed in 1903. A much-praised equestrian sculpture, the monument depicts General Tecumseh Sherman led by a winged figure of Victory. At his studio in
Cornish, New Hampshire, Saint-Gaudens revised the
head of Victory several times, even while the monument was being cast. He later produced bronze casts,
including this one, of the head's second version.
Noted American artist Kenyon Cox wrote of the Victory figure on the Sherman Monument: "She has a certain fierce wildness of aspect, but her rapt gaze and
half-open mouth indicate the seer of visions[:] peace
is ahead and an end of war."

Dying Centaur

William Rimmer (1816–1879)

New York, New York, 1869

Plaster

The powerful musculature and complex pose of the *Dying Centaur* reveal William Rimmer's unusual background as a physician and self-taught artist. The son of a cobbler who believed he was a lost descendant of French royalty, Rimmer grew up in Boston, where he displayed an early aptitude for art and dabbled in a variety of trades. While pursuing a painting career as a young man, he studied anatomy and soon began his own practice as a self-taught physician in Brockton and later in Milton, Massachusetts. His early and untutored experiments in sculpture caught the attention of Stephen H. Perkins, a wealthy Boston patron who came to champion Rimmer's career. Rimmer soon gained a measure of fame as a sculptor and art teacher noted for his understanding of human anatomy.

Dying Centaur depicts a familiar mythological subject without the classical restraint and calm of contemporary Neoclassical sculpture. Rimmer portrayed the sprawling figure in a moment of physical and spiritual anguish, one truncated arm extended heavenward as if imploring aid from the gods. The figure's raw emotion may reflect the influence of French artist Antoine-Louis Barye's romantic and violent animal sculptures, popular at this time. The work may also be an autobiographical statement about Rimmer's own melancholy, expressing his feelings of isolation and disappointment at the lack of adequate recognition during his lifetime. Immediately after his death, the Rimmer Memorial Committee selected *Dying Centaur* as the first of his compositions to be cast in bronze, and in 1880 the Museum of Fine Arts, Boston, held an important memorial exhibition of the artist's work.

H. 53.3 cm, w. 68.6 cm, d. 61 cm (H. 21 in., w. 27 in., d. 24 in.)
Bequest of Miss Caroline Hunt Rimmer   RES.19.127

Punch bowl and ladle

Gorham Manufacturing Company (active 1865–1961)

Providence, Rhode Island, 1885

Silver

The United States' westward expansion, global trade, and booming industrial economy in the late nineteenth century set the stage for the creation of large and lavish silver objects like this punch bowl and ladle set. Silver was more plentiful and more affordable than ever before following the discovery of large silver deposits in western territories and the dramatic reduction in the price of silver when the U.S. government changed to the currency standard in 1873. Grand silver objects symbolizing American ambition became important emblems for the nation's wealthy elite, who practiced what economist Thorstein Veblen, in his 1849 *The Theory of the Leisure Class,* famously called "conspicuous consumption."

The Japanesque style of the handwrought ornament on the punch bowl and ladle reflect America's transformation into a global imperial power. After Commodore Matthew Perry forcibly opened Japan to trade in 1854 and vast quantities of Japanese objects were exported to the West for the first time in centuries, American artists and designers became fascinated with Japanese aesthetics. Japonisme, a style that hybridized Japanese and Western decoration, was widespread in the 1870s and 1880s and was used with particular success in metalwork by the firms Tiffany and Company and Gorham Manufacturing Company. The naturalistic rendering of living creatures, especially insects, birds, and sea life became an important element of this style. The undulating surfaces of the punch bowl and ladle present an extravagant display of bountiful aquatic life in a loosely asymmetrical, Japanese-derived style. Corals and sponges at the base of the bowl indicate the ocean floor, and the rim is encrusted with sand, crabs, seaweed, and shells representing the seashore.

Punch bowl: H. 25.7 cm, w. 38.7 cm, diam. rim 23.5 cm, diam. foot 17.8 cm, wt. 3500 gm (H. 10⅛ in., w. 15¼ in., diam. rim 9¼ in., diam. foot 7 in., wt. 112 oz. 10 dwt. 13 gr.)
Ladle: L. 35.6 cm, w. bowl 9.5 cm, wt. 241.3 gm
(L. 14 in., w. bowl 3¾ in., wt. 7 oz. 15 dwt. 4 gr.)
Edwin E. Jack Fund   1980.383–384

Peonies Blown in the Wind

John La Farge (1835–1910)

New York, New York, 1886

Stained glass

The mid-nineteenth-century Gothic Revival, which sparked an interest in medieval arts, and the Aesthetic Movement of the 1870s and 1880s, which emphasized artistic unity in interior decoration, both popularized and secularized stained glass and elevated its importance as an art form. Although the majority of stained glass used in the United States was imported from England and made in a traditional manner, American artists John La Farge and Louis Comfort Tiffany separately, yet simultaneously, experimented with new techniques and designs that offered remarkable, unconventional qualities of texture and color.

La Farge's most important contribution to the art of stained glass was his use of opalescent glass (which he claimed to have invented) in multiple layers to create variegated hues and dramatic effects of depth. Unlike traditional stained glass, in which the artist painted the flat surface to render details and shading, La Farge's windows achieve the effects of shading and three-dimensionality through the layering and shaping of the glass itself. For greater textural effect, he often used an outer layer that had a corrugated appearance produced by compressing or stamping sheets of hot glass. Many of his works incorporated chunks or pebbles of glass — or even cut, faceted glass nuggets — to refract light, as seen in the jewel-like border of this example.

This extraordinary window, one of five incorporating the Japanese-inspired peony design, was made for the studio of British painter Lawrence Alma-Tadema. Jean Guiffrey, a former curator at the Louvre who helped the MFA acquire the window in 1913, wrote that "La Farge has worked out the shape and

shading of every one of the flowers' delicate petals solely by this process of varying the thickness of the glass. Before this could be done, he had first to sculpture the flowers and then make his final design in glass from the original carved model. It was work requiring the rarest technique and skill."

H. 180.3 cm, w. 101.6 cm (H. 71 in., w. 40 in.)

General Funds 13.2802

Cabinet

Herter Brothers (active 1865–1905)
New York, New York, about 1880
Maple, bird's-eye maple, oak or chestnut, stamped and
gilt paper, with gilding, inlay, and carved decoration;
original brass pulls and key

Representing the highest level of art furniture, this
elegant cabinet expresses the vocabulary of the
Japanesque taste in a rich variety of materials. Its
spare and linear form is Neoclassical in character,
but its rectilinear design is enlivened by asymmetrical ornament derived from such sources as Japanese
screens and woodblock prints. As on the Gorham
punch bowl (p. 151), the marquetry decoration of the
cabinet celebrates Japanese naturalistic ornament.
The panels depict extraordinarily detailed insect and
plant life, including tiny beetles munching holes in
the leaves on the top panel. Another striking feature is
the stamped and stenciled gilt paper that lines the
niches and splashboard. Several furniture makers,
including Herter Brothers, used textiles to line
shelves and niches on furniture in this period, but
elaborate paper used in this manner rarely survived.
The gold paper, embossed with an intricate pattern,
was stenciled with reddish-brown flowers scattered
irregularly across the surface.
The flowers vary in size and
shape, rhythmically echo-
ing the floral motifs of the
carved and inlaid panels.

Herter Brothers, headed by Gustav Herter and his
half brother Christian, produced some of New York's
finest furniture in a rich and eclectic array of styles in
the post–Civil War period. A pencil inscription on the
back of this cabinet reads "N. 908 Harriman Esq.,"
suggesting that it may have been made for financier
Edward Henry Harriman. Harriman made his money
at a young age on Wall Street and in railroads, and
was described by contemporaries as both "dashing"
and "cold and ruthless." Although his ownership of
the cabinet is not certain, the piece represents the
costly, sometimes one-of-a-kind designs that Herter
Brothers produced for Harriman's peers, the robber-
baron elite.

H. 133.4 cm, w. 184.8 cm, d. 38.4 cm
(H. 52½ in., w. 72¾ in., d. 15⅛ in.)
Museum purchase with funds donated anonymously and
the Frank B. Bemis Fund   2000.3

REACTION AND REFORM: the late nineteenth and early twentieth centuries

Reaction and Reform: The Late Nineteenth and Early Twentieth Centuries Nonie Gadsden

Reform movements swept through the United States in the late nineteenth century, transforming labor, business, alcohol consumption, women's rights, and more. Art and design did not escape this scrutiny; in fact they played a key role in the perceived solution. Design reformers and other leaders believed that a better aesthetic environment would improve society as a whole. To many, good art encouraged good behavior.

fig. 26. Sara Galner decorates the wares at the Paul Revere Pottery, about 1915. Photograph courtesy of Dr. David L. Bloom and family.

The writings of such British theorists as John Ruskin and William Morris sparked the most influential, international design-reform philosophy of this period, the Arts and Crafts Movement. These reformers denounced mass-manufactured "machine art" and the dehumanizing effect of factory life. Encouraging a return to beauty through hand-craftsmanship and the study of nature, they evoked an idealized vision of communal medieval life and ancient guild practices that advocated "honest" construction and "truth to materials." As these ideas spread globally, it became clear that the Arts and Crafts Movement was a lifestyle and design philosophy rather than a specific artistic style. Individual artisans or groups emphasized some tenets of the movement over others, depending on their nation's or region's current challenges. Some focused on finding peace and harmony through the complete integration of art and life. Others integrated design motifs and craft techniques from the region's ethnic heritage to encourage unity and national identity.

Arts and Crafts ideals attracted many Americans who were disenchanted with industrialized society and the busy, highly decorated aesthetic of the late nineteenth century. The Society of Arts and Crafts, Boston (SACB), formed in 1897, was the first of many such organizations that sprang up across the nation. The society pledged in its bylaws to "develop and encourage higher artistic standards in the handicrafts" through mentoring, educational efforts, and exhibitions in which members displayed and sold their wares. Other Arts and Crafts devotees concentrated on the potential of social reform through craft training. Dr. Herbert J. Hall established the Marblehead Pottery in Massachusetts to provide occupational therapy for patients suffering from nervous disorders. Jane Addams's Hull House in Chicago and the Saturday Evening Girls club in Boston both used crafts to assimilate and offer opportunities to immigrants and the poor (fig. 26). Similarly, crafts offered women an acceptable activity outside the home and perhaps even a source of income. Some potteries, including Rookwood in Cincinnati and Newcomb in New Orleans, started as china-painting ventures for genteel women.

Several Americans took the radical step of pursuing William Morris's vision of utopian artist communities in idyllic natural settings. Often founded by wealthy idealists, these communities achieved mixed success, depending on their source of funding and skill in marketing their wares. Ralph and Jane Whitehead's Byrdcliffe community in Woodstock, New York, struggled despite its reputation as a vibrant center for the exchange of ideas. Elbert Hubbard's Roycroft in East Aurora, New York, enjoyed more success through mass advertising, although the artisans were only allowed to create a limited range of designs. In embracing modern marketing and machines, Hubbard—like some of his contemporaries, including Arts and Crafts guru Gustav Stickley—broke with English doctrine but achieved a high rate of financial success and promoted the Arts and Crafts lifestyle to a wide audience.

As the movement spread throughout the country, regional interpretations arose, with philosophical and stylistic variations. Boston and the Northeast served as the movement's intellectual hub in the United States. New England artists came closest to the romantic visions of British proponents, including the utopian communities and their strong emphasis on mining the past for aesthetic inspiration. Architect Henry Hobson Richardson's work on Trinity Church, Boston, was a key forerunner of the American Arts and Crafts Movement; Richardson used a modernized medieval Romanesque style of architecture and collaborated with a talented group of artisans to create unified, artistic interior spaces and furnishings. A later generation of American architects and designers including Ralph Adams Cram and Elizabeth Copeland continued to experiment with and draw upon medieval European styles. Others were inspired by American designs of the eighteenth century, creating the Colonial Revival style, a nostalgic if errant interpretation of colonial life as simple, pure, and pastoral. New England silver-

fig. 27. (opposite page)
Tall-back side chair, designed
by Frank Lloyd Wright
(1867–1959) for the Warren
Hickox House, 1900; made by
John W. Ayers & Co. (1890–1913),
Chicago, Illinois, about 1900.
Courtesy of American
Decorative Art 1900 Foundation.

smith Arthur Stone updated historic American designs, often simplifying his Colonial Revival style so much that it looked starkly modern.

Architects in the Midwest who absorbed Arts and Crafts ideas, including Frank Lloyd Wright and George Washington Maher, developed a related modern, rectilinear style (fig. 27). The Prairie School, whose distinctive style reflected the low horizontal lines of the landscape, espoused the total unification of architecture and interior design with its natural setting, using color, texture, and repetitive patterns. The Midwest's relative lack of historic precedent allowed these artisans the freedom to experiment and explore the work of other cultures, among them the geometric patterns of design reform leaders in Vienna and the asymmetrical compositions of Japanese artists.

Many artists moved from the Northeast and the Midwest to the West Coast, particularly California, in search of a healthy lifestyle and mild climate. These artisans often included in their work elements of the area's Spanish or Mexican heritage, or emphasized the region's spectacular natural attributes. While regional Arts and Crafts guilds helped to promote the movement's ideals, most California artisans worked individually or in small shops, forging their own unique stylistic identities.

American Arts and Crafts enthusiasts looked both to the past and the future. The range of social ideas and artistic styles associated with the movement reflects the diversity of the country and the freedom of artisans to express themselves. The movement's philosophical focus on the individual artist and handcraftsmanship persisted in the development of the studio craft movement in the second half of the twentieth century.

Armchair

Possibly manufactured by A. H. Davenport and
Company (1841–1973); designed by Henry Hobson Richardson
(1838–1886)

Probably Boston, Massachusetts, 1878

Oak, leather

One of America's most influential architects of the nineteenth century, Henry Hobson Richardson is best known for his original interpretation of early medieval building styles in modern architecture; he himself described the style as "a free rendering of the French Romanesque." As an important figure in the design-reform movement of the period, he designed furnishings and interiors integrated with the overall architectural scheme of his libraries, churches, and other public buildings. For the Woburn Public Library (sometimes called Winn Memorial Library) in Woburn, Massachusetts—the first of several public library commissions, constructed from 1876 to 1879—Richardson designed this chair to harmonize with the curved lines of the wooden barrel-vaulted ceiling in the book room and the picturesque, neo-medieval style of the building.

The chair reveals the influence of British architects and design reformers, including Augustus Welby Northmore Pugin, Bruce Talbert, William Morris, and others who advocated a return to the "honest" design principles of medieval furniture. Richardson intended its solid oak frame with chamfered, or angled, edges and deliberately exposed joinery to suggest the sturdy character of medieval furniture so admired by the English reformers. The chair's curving, crossed members and pared-down structure may be indebted to Gothic-inspired designs by Pugin and Talbert, including X-frame chairs and tables. Nevertheless, Richardson's chair was an original form, that, despite its massive scale, is visually lightened by its spare carved ornament and its unusual cantilevered arms.

H. 85.4 cm, w. 74.9 cm, d. 71.1 cm (H. 33⅝ in., w. 29½ in., d. 28 in.)
Gift of Woburn Public Library 61.236

Pitcher

**Rookwood Pottery Company (1880–1967); decorated
by Constance Amelia Baker (active 1892–1904);
Gorham Manufacturing Company (1865–1961)**

Cincinnati, Ohio (ceramic), and Providence, Rhode
Island (silver), 1893

White earthenware with polychrome glaze, silver

The Rookwood Pottery was one of the earliest and
most successful art potteries in the United States.
Amateur artist and heiress Maria Longworth
Nichols established Rookwood in 1880 after admir-
ing the high quality of Japanese and Chinese ceramics at the Philadelphia Centennial Exposition of
1876. She wanted to create an "art industry" to encourage creativity, experimentation, and beauty in
American manufacturing. From its beginnings as a
small workshop where wealthy women and other
amateurs painted simple shapes, the pottery evolved
into a large-scale producer of many different styles
and patterns.

By 1883, Nichols hired William Watts Taylor to
manage Rookwood. Within several years Taylor had transformed the operation into a
profit-making commercial venture. He
developed a standard glaze of earth tones
and marketed the pottery as fine art,
emphasized by artist signatures on each
piece. This pitcher, painted with a blend
of warm brown, yellow, red, and green and
signed "CAB" by decorator Constance
Amelia Baker, is an excellent example of
"Standard Rookwood." In addition, this piece
is embellished with swirling silver overlay
by the Gorham Manufacturing Company.
Rookwood forged a relationship

with Gorham in an attempt to enliven its wares for
the 1893 World's Columbian Exposition in Chicago.
The collaboration was short-lived, perhaps because
the painted designs and the silver ornament rarely
complemented one another, as illustrated by the com-
peting floral and vegetal motifs on this pitcher.

H. 16.8 cm, w. 20.9 cm, d. 15.2 cm
(H. 6⅝ in., w. 8¼ in., d. 6 in.)
Edwin E. Jack Fund 1989.200

Cabinet

Byrdcliffe Arts and Crafts Colony furniture shop (active
1902–1905); designed by Edna Walker (born 1880)
Woodstock, New York, 1902–5
Oak with polychrome stained and carved panels, yellow poplar,
original brass hardware

In founding the Byrdcliffe Arts and
Crafts Colony in 1902, Ralph Radcliffe
Whitehead and Jane Byrd McCall Whitehead sought to foster creative artistic collaboration and experimentation in an idyllic
setting. They built rustic cabins in the
Catskill Mountains of Woodstock, New York,
and invited writers, painters, photographers,
and craftspeople to use them as workshops
and studios. The Whiteheads financed the
start of the colony, hoping that craft sales
would ultimately support the community.

Although some of the workshops profited,
the furniture enterprise failed, closing in
1905. Fewer than fifty pieces were produced,
including this massive dark-stained cabinet.
The piece's simple, rectilinear form and solid
construction adhere to the Arts and Crafts
principles promoted by the Whiteheads, and
the naturalistic carved decoration on the
doors lightens its visual weight. The flowering tulip poplar motif is accented with trans-
parent stains that allow the grain of the
wood to show through, adding organic
rhythm and movement to the design. Two
related drawings survive (also in the MFA):
one illustrating the cabinet's form and one
outlining the tulip poplar panel design. Both
are signed by Edna Walker, a trained artist
who joined the Byrdcliffe community in the
summer of 1903.

H. 184.8 cm, w. 138.7, d. 63.2 cm (H. 72¾ in., w. 54⅝ in., d. 24⅞ in.)
Museum purchase with funds donated anonymously and Frank B. Bemis
Fund   2003.61

Hanging lantern

Roycroft Community (1895–1938); designed by Dard
Hunter (1883–1966); made by Karl Kipp (1882–1954)

East Aurora, New York, about 1903–8

Copper, nickel silver, stained glass, leather

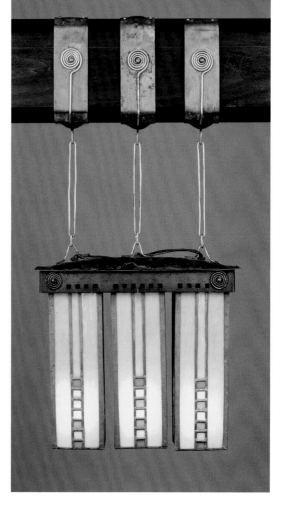

Unfulfilled by running a soap company in Buffalo,
New York, Elbert Hubbard quit his job and searched
for inspiration, first at Harvard, then on a walking
tour of England. Hubbard found his muse when he
visited William Morris's Kelmscott Press, which produced beautiful, artful editions of Morris's own writings, and works by the leading authors of the period.
Stimulated by Morris's ideas, Hubbard returned to
the United States, founded a printing press to publish
his own writings and established Roycroft, a utopian
artist community in East Aurora, New York. Hubbard's charismatic personality attracted talented
artisans to his workshops, while his business acu-
men promoted their wares using mass-marketing
methods.

This three-light lantern is one of twelve that hung
in the dining hall of the Roycroft Inn, built in 1903 for
visitors who came to observe and purchase goods
from the community. Designed by Dard Hunter and
made by Karl Kipp, head of the Roycroft Copper Shop,
the lantern illustrates the strong Viennese influence
on many of Roycroft's products. Hunter, a young and
talented designer, eagerly studied English and German publications, which included the work of the
budding Vienna Secession. This exposure is evident in
the geometric design of the lantern, accented by glass
squares of varying colors.

H. 76.2 cm, w. 40.6 cm, d. 15.2 cm (H. 30 in., w. 16 in., d. 6 in.)
Harriet Otis Cruft Fund   1980.279

Tile

Grueby Faience Company (1894–1909) or Grueby Faience and Tile Company (1909–1919); designed by Addison B. LeBoutillier (1872–1951)

Boston, Massachusetts, about 1906–19
Pressed and glazed earthenware

Ceramics innovator William H. Grueby's style of "organic naturalism" transformed the direction of art pottery in the United States and abroad. His vegetal forms are articulated by subtle tooling and finished with opaque, dripping glazes that blurred the line between form and surface decoration. Although best known today for three-dimensional forms, Grueby began his career making architectural tiles. Tiles remained the foundation of his company's production, and a new line of interior Arts and Crafts–inspired decorative tiles introduced about 1902 reinvigorated the company's flagging sales. Grueby's new designer, illustrator Addison B. LeBoutillier, created the line using flat, stylized designs of flowers, trees, animals, and ships that reduced the image to abstract pattern.

This large tile is adapted from an eight-tile frieze LeBoutillier designed in 1906 called "The Pines." Using an ancient Moorish process, the clay was impressed with the design, forming channels with low walls that kept Grueby's characteristic thick glazes separate. The tile combines LeBoutillier's drafting skills with Grueby's variety of color tone and texture, resulting in a stylized scene with a soft surface that typifies the best works of the Arts and Crafts Movement.

H. 31.1 cm, w. 31.1 cm, d. 2.5 cm (H. 12¼ in., w. 12¼ in., d. 1 in.)
Anonymous gift in memory of John G. Pierce   65.215

"Stalking Panther" bowl

Marblehead Pottery (1904–1936)

Marblehead, Massachusetts, 1910–15

Wheel-thrown earthenware with incised and glazed decoration

In 1904, Dr. Herbert J. Hall established the Marblehead Pottery to provide occupational therapy to patients suffering from nervous exhaustion and depression. The therapeutic mission soon gave way to commercial pressures as the small pottery sought to enforce quality control. In 1905, Hall hired Arthur E. Baggs, a formally trained potter and glaze chemist who would take over as director in 1908. Baggs developed Marblehead's signature style of simple hand-thrown shapes, matte glazes with pebbled grounds, and conventionalized decoration. The vast majority of the pottery's production was basic commercial wares that fulfilled Baggs's standards of quality but had no additional adornment. Today, the rarer ornamented pots are renowned for their restrained decoration in the Arts and Crafts manner.

The "Stalking Panther" bowl, with its complex design, rich tones, and exotic panther motif, is an exceptional example of the pottery's elite production. Most works combined subtle, cool colors and austere, highly regimented, or geometric patterns. On this piece, the strong horizontal band of the design is regularly punctuated by vertical bars around which slink the shadowy figures. The flat, graphic design is further enlivened by the pulsing yellow background. Although it is unclear whether Baggs himself made this unusual piece, the bowl descended in his family with the story that the potter gave it to his wife as a present.

H. 9.8 cm, diam. 27.3 cm (H. 3⅞ in., diam. 10¾ in.)

Gift of John P. Axelrod 1990.508

Vase

Designed by Arthur Stone (1847–1938);
made by Herbert A. Taylor (active 1908–1937)
Gardner, Massachusetts, 1914
Silver

Arthur Stone was perhaps one of the United States' most important silversmiths of the Arts and Crafts era. Born in England and trained through the traditional apprentice system, Stone also took evening courses on design. He became a strong proponent of William Morris's Arts and Crafts principles, and his search to implement those ideals brought him to the United States in 1884. After working for commercial retailers, Stone opened his own shop in Gardner, Massachusetts, in 1901.

As the head of his shop, Stone was finally able to put his theories on collaborative craftsmanship and healthy working conditions into practice. He mentored his employees, teaching them secrets of the craft, encouraging their study of past cultures at the Museum of Fine Arts and other institutions, and sponsoring their membership in the Society of Arts and Crafts, Boston. He allowed artisans to add their mark next to his on the pieces they created, and he shared the workshop's profits with his employees on a semiannual basis.

An active member of the SACB, Stone was widely admired for his leadership and pioneering efforts and for his restrained designs that many called expressly "American." He looked to both the European and American past for inspiration, enhancing his knowledge of historic styles by studying the collections of the MFA, including taking measurements and reproducing some works. This vase reflects Stone's careful study: its vertical fluting is borrowed from the early Baroque style; wispy flowers and tracery are expressive of the sinuous Art Nouveau style; and the bold, jewel-like medallions evoke medieval works. These ornamental elements also complement the shape of the vase, accentuating its vertical thrust and subtle swelling toward the rim.

H. 19.7 cm, diam. 11.2 cm, wt. 521.9 gm
(H. 7¹³/₁₆ in., diam. 4⅜ in., wt. 16 oz. 15 dwt. 14 gr.)
Seth K. Sweetser Fund   1978.234

fig. 28. **Studio of Arthur Stone, Gardner, Massachusetts, about** 1908.

Tea caddy

Saturday Evening Girls, Paul Revere Pottery (1908–1942); painted by Sara Galner (1894–1982)

Boston, Massachusetts, 1914

Earthenware

H. 11.1 cm, w. 7.6 cm, d. 8.9 cm (H. 4⅜ in., w. 3 in., d. 3½ in.)

Promised gift of Dr. David L. Bloom and family in memory of his mother Sara Galner Bloom

Goose bowl

Saturday Evening Girls, Paul Revere Pottery (1908–1942); painted by Sara Galner (1894–1982)

Boston, Massachusetts, 1914

Earthenware

H. 12.7 cm, diam. 29.5 cm (H. 5 in., diam. 11⅝ in.)

Promised gift of Dr. David L. Bloom and family in memory of his mother Sara Galner Bloom

Rabbit bowl

Saturday Evening Girls, Paul Revere Pottery (1908–1942)

Boston, Massachusetts, 1908

Earthenware

H. 3.8 cm, diam. 15.6 cm (H. 1½ in., diam. 6⅛ in.)

Promised gift of Dr. David L. Bloom and family in memory of his mother Sara Galner Bloom

The Paul Revere Pottery was established in Boston's North End in 1908 under the direction of Edith Guerrier and her artistic partner, Edith Brown. Guerrier ran the neighborhood's branch of the Boston Public Library and had developed educational clubs for local immigrant girls, primarily of Italian and Eastern European heritage. The clubs were part of a citywide effort to keep these girls "off the streets" and to assimilate them into the American way of life. Financed by philanthropist Helen Osborne Storrow, the pottery's mission was to help support the library clubs and to offer the oldest girls, members of the Saturday Evening Girls (SEG) club, an opportunity to earn money in a healthy and stimulating work environment. The child's bowl—decorated with rabbits, turtles, and the advice "The race is not always to the swift"—is one of the earliest known works produced by the pottery and shows the early, gritty surfaces that were soon replaced with high-gloss glazes.

Sara Galner, a Jewish immigrant from Austria-Hungary, joined the SEG library club in her early teens, hiding her books from her disapproving parents. Galner joined the pottery in its nascent years and continued to work there until her marriage in 1921, occasionally running the pottery's retail stores in downtown Boston and Washington, D.C. Her painted designs reveal the pottery's shifts in glazes, color palettes, and patterns, and her own maturation as a decorator. Identified by her initials on the base, the large bowl featuring animated geese, and the detailed tea caddy, which seems to tell a story about the rural cottage surrounded by trees, are among the finest examples of both Galner's and the pottery's work.

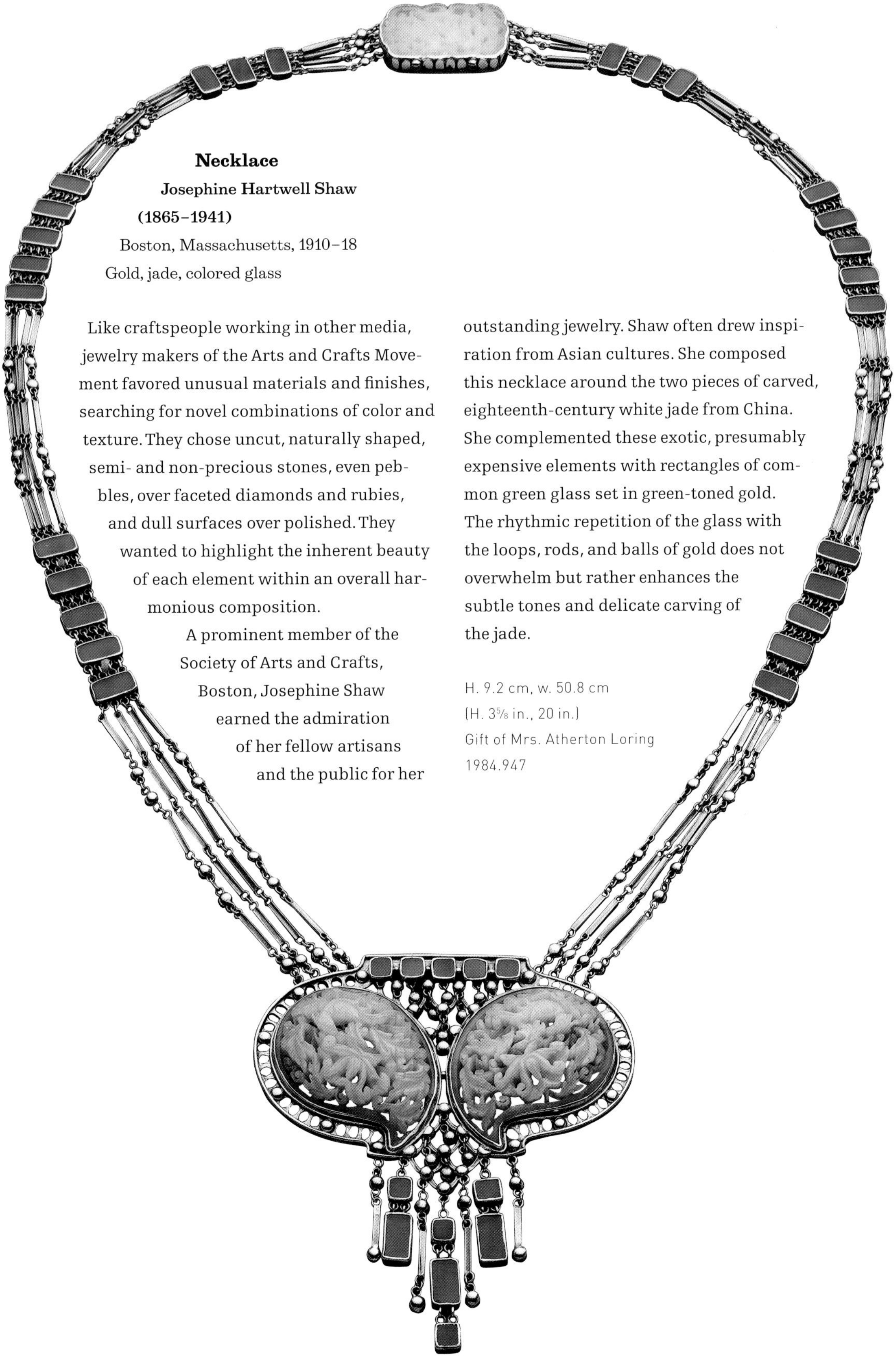

Necklace

Josephine Hartwell Shaw

(1865–1941)

Boston, Massachusetts, 1910–18

Gold, jade, colored glass

Like craftspeople working in other media, jewelry makers of the Arts and Crafts Movement favored unusual materials and finishes, searching for novel combinations of color and texture. They chose uncut, naturally shaped, semi- and non-precious stones, even pebbles, over faceted diamonds and rubies, and dull surfaces over polished. They wanted to highlight the inherent beauty of each element within an overall harmonious composition.

A prominent member of the Society of Arts and Crafts, Boston, Josephine Shaw earned the admiration of her fellow artisans and the public for her outstanding jewelry. Shaw often drew inspiration from Asian cultures. She composed this necklace around the two pieces of carved, eighteenth-century white jade from China. She complemented these exotic, presumably expensive elements with rectangles of common green glass set in green-toned gold. The rhythmic repetition of the glass with the loops, rods, and balls of gold does not overwhelm but rather enhances the subtle tones and delicate carving of the jade.

H. 9.2 cm, w. 50.8 cm
(H. 3⅝ in., 20 in.)
Gift of Mrs. Atherton Loring
1984.947

Child's bed

William F. Ross and Company,
cabinetmakers (active about 1904–1921);
designed by Ralph Adams Cram (1863–1942);
carved by John Kirchmayer (1860–1930)
Boston, Massachusetts, about 1913
Walnut with polychrome and gilt decoration, oak

Although Arts and Crafts rhetoric espoused morality, honesty, and simplicity, the movement was not explicitly associated with religion. Its secular spirituality attracted many followers, and others blended their own religious beliefs into the Arts and Crafts lifestyle and their creations. Architect Ralph Adams Cram, a devout Catholic renowned for his church buildings, was one of the founding members of the Society of Arts and Crafts, Boston. Like many Bostonians, Cram looked to the arts of the Middle Ages for inspiration and was particularly drawn to the

ecclesiastical style of the era, the Gothic. In his reform Gothic Revival designs, Cram experimented with merging the old and the new; he sought to create works "in a medieval spirit vitalized by modern conditions."

This combination is seen in domestic scale in the bed Cram designed for his daughter Elizabeth. The labor-intensive panel-and-frame construction and hand-carved ornament evoke the craftsmanship of the Middle Ages. Yet the Gothic lettering of the biblical inscription and the painted and gilt guardian angels at each corner of the bed frame introduce an abstract quality that suggests the modern. The carved elements of the bed were executed by Boston's leading carver of the Arts and Crafts period, John (Johannes) Kirchmayer. A frequent collaborator of Cram's, Kirchmayer emigrated from Germany in the 1890s and quickly became known for the quality and distinctive style of his religious carvings. The bed's angels are a provocative mix of distinctive facial features and stylized, abstract bodies and clothing. Originally made as a crib with vertical slats on the sides, the piece was modified into a youth's bed as Elizabeth grew.

H. 201.9 cm, w. 94 cm, d. 193 cm (H. 79½ in., w. 37 in., d. 76 in.)
Gift of David W. Scudder and Judith S. Robinson in memory of their grandfather, Ralph Adams Cram 1997.210

Candlestick

Elizabeth Ethel Copeland (1866–1957)

Boston, Massachusetts, 1917

Silver, enamel

Women from a variety of economic backgrounds took advantage of the Arts and Crafts Movement's focus on household wares as an opportunity to learn craft skills and enter the work force. Elizabeth Copeland, a single woman living with family members, broke away from her domestic chores to begin her studies at the Cowles Art School in Boston at the age of thirty-four. From 1900 to 1904 she commuted into the city three times a week from her hometown of Revere to study design and learn handicraft skills, including metalworking.

Her decision to concentrate on the traditionally male-dominated art of enamel, however, set Copeland apart. The labor-intensive craft required a furnace, forcing its practitioners to work outside the home and subjecting them to uncomfortable working conditions with extreme heat. Yet Copeland excelled and quickly gained recognition for her enameled jewelry and metalwork. Before long, she was able to support herself by selling her wares.

Copeland, like many of her contemporaries in Boston, looked to the past for inspiration. She is best known today for her enameled boxes in the medieval style, though her jewelry earned equal praise during her life. This rare candlestick (the only known example) combines Copeland's interest in the medieval with her intense love of color. The bright purple-blues and greens that cover the base give a playful tone to the traditional form of the piece.

H. 18.7 cm, w. 10.5 cm, d. 10.5 cm
(H. 7⅜ in., w. 4⅛ in., d. 4⅛ in.)
Gift of The Seminarians in honor of J. E. Robinson III
1997.56

Punch bowl

Clemens Friedell (1872–1963)

Pasadena, California, about 1912

Silver

Clemens Friedell opened a shop in Pasadena in 1911 and quickly gained a reputation as one of California's top silversmiths. Previously he had belonged to an elite group of artisans, working as a skilled decorator called a "chaser" at the Gorham Company in Providence, Rhode Island. His experience producing Gorham's sinuous and highly ornamented "Martelé" wares in the Art Nouveau fashion is evident in his later independent style. Friedell's designs merged hallmarks of the Arts and Crafts Movement, among them the visible hammer marks that emphasize handcraftsmanship, with the flowing curves and visual depth of the Art Nouveau style. His decorative objects often incorporated native California flora, such as orange blossoms or poppies, in vivid three-dimensional relief. Large golden poppies, the state flower and most common ornament of California Arts and Crafts artisans, embellish this enormous punch bowl, made as a trophy for the Hogan Challenge Polo tournament about 1912. The bowl may be the "huge punch bowl" that Friedell later exhibited at the 1915 Panama-California Exhibition in San Diego, for which he received a gold medal.

H. 36.2 cm, diam. rim 45.1 cm, diam. base 26 cm, wt. 3234 gm (H. 14¼ in., diam. rim 17¾ in., diam. base 10¼ in., wt. 103 oz. 19 dwt. 12 gr.)
Museum purchase with funds donated anonymously, and from Shirley and Walter Amory, John and Catherine Coolidge Lastavica, the H. E. Bolles Fund, the Michaelson Family Trust, James G. Hinkle, Jr. and Roy Hammer, Robert Rosenberg, Sue Schenck, the Grace and Floyd Lee Bell Fund, and Miklos Toth   2003.730

Rocking chair

George Washington Maher (1864–1926)

Kenilworth, Illinois, about 1912

Oak, modern leather upholstery

George Washington Maher and his fellow Prairie School architects designed low, horizontal houses with long banks of windows, overhanging roofs, and coordinated furnishings. Maher took the concept of unified design even further than his contemporaries with his "motif rhythm theory," which advocated the use of a limited number of repeated elements to "bind the design together." He argued that the specific motifs should be individualized to the home, drawn from the local landscape or personal interests of his client.

Rockledge, a summer residence built in 1912 along the Mississippi River in Homer, Minnesota, was an exemplary manifestation of Maher's theory. His chosen motifs included a segmented arch and trapezoidal guttae (an ornamental architectural detail)—simple, geometric shapes that did not overwhelm or distract from the overall design. These subtle elements reveal his exposure to and interest in the linear and geometric work of avant-garde European designers of the Vienna Secession and Wiener Werkstätte.

For this rocker's design, Maher used the segmented arch for the crest rail and arm supports, and trapezoidal guttae as decorative capitals on vertical posts. The imposing, architectonic form is emphasized by the wide base, tapering front-facing posts, and cornice moldings. Maher even chose the greenish brown stain of the oak to harmonize with the overall color scheme of the home, a mixture of earth tones that complemented the natural setting.

H. 94 cm, w. 69.9 cm, d. 85.1 cm (H. 37 in., w. 27½ in., d. 33½ in.)
William E. Nickerson Fund 1984.20

Jeweled casket

Edward Everett Oakes (1891–1960)

Boston, Massachusetts, 1929
Silver, green gold, amethysts, Japanese pearls, Oriental
pearls, onyx, laurel wood

In 1926, Boston jeweler Edward Everett Oakes mused
that he "dream[ed] of leaving a single magnificent
work to compare favorably with the great jewelers of
the Renaissance." Shortly after expressing this wish,
Oakes began designing and gathering materials to
create this extraordinary jeweled casket. The Society
of Arts and Crafts, Boston, exhibited Oakes's masterpiece to great acclaim from his colleagues, the press,
and the public. One writer called the piece "architecture in miniature," while Boston architect Ralph
Adams Cram proclaimed the casket to be "an extraordinary piece, not only of goldsmith craft but of original design."

By the time he made this tour de force, Oakes was
already established as a talented craftsman working
in historic styles. He had learned how to make jewelry
from fellow members of the SACB, Frank Gardner
Hale and Josephine Hartwell Shaw. His Arts and
Crafts training is evident in the medieval casket form
and the restrained foliate decoration of the jewel
mounts. Yet Oakes also incorporated elements of the
modern Art Deco style, seen in his extravagant use of
precious stones (the piece boasts 143 amethysts, 18
Japanese pearls, 68 Oriental pearls, and 88 onyx) and
in the stepped, skyscraper-like designs at the casket
corners. Oakes's hopes that the piece would be
acquired for the MFA following its unveiling in October 1929 were dashed days after the event by the stock
market crash. The casket remained in the family, and
his wish finally came true nearly seventy years later.

H. 13.5 cm, w. 20.2 cm, d. 16 cm
(H. 5⁵⁄₁₆ in., w. 7¹⁵⁄₁₆ in., d. 6⁵⁄₁₆ in.)
Museum purchase with funds donated anonymously
2000.628.1–2

Modernism and Design: The Early and Mid-Twentieth Century

Kelly H. L'Ecuyer

In the opening decades of the twentieth century, Americans grappled with the consequences of a fully industrialized society. The economic growth and rapid urbanization of the late nineteenth century had brought prosperity to wealthy industrialists and a growing middle class, but had also contributed to overcrowded slums, pollution, and labor unrest. Some sought refuge from such modern complexities in a nostalgic view of the supposedly simpler values of the preindustrial past, popularly expressed in the Colonial Revival movement or, more progressively, in the Arts and Crafts Movement. Others, in contrast, celebrated the improved standards of living brought by the machine age: affordable automobiles, mass transit, electrified homes, and better consumer products. While Colonial Revival entrepreneurs like Wallace Nutting found a ready market for nostalgia, modernists in all fields of the arts sought to create works that addressed twentieth-century life on its own terms.

The international Art Deco style that emerged after World War I encompassed a variety of sources and expressions symbolizing all that was new, glamorous, and modern. Named for the acclaimed Paris Exposition Internationale des Arts Décoratifs et Industriels Modernes of 1925, the style spanned the Roaring Twenties and the Depression years of the 1930s. Art Deco designers used abstract forms and rhythmic geometric patterns to convey the energy and excitement of the machine age in decorative arts objects. Like avant-garde painters and sculptors many years earlier, designers looked to so-called "primitive" sources such as African masks, American folk art, and the art of ancient civilizations in Egypt, Greece, and Mexico. They admired the simplified forms, direct expression, and visual energy of these nonacademic arts, and sought to incorporate these qualities into designs for the modern age. Sleek, stylized animals, inspired by folk art and various ancient sources, recurred frequently in Art Deco designs, including graphically printed furnishing fabrics (fig. 29).

Although they drew ideas from "primitive" art, designers also borrowed from high-style European decorative arts, especially furniture in the classical taste of the late eighteenth and early nineteenth century. By adapting the clean geometric lines and refined surface ornament of this style, Art Deco designers created modern furniture with an air of French sophistication for stylish urban consumers. The armoire made by the Company of Master Craftsmen for the furniture retailer W. and J. Sloane, for example, translated eighteenth-century French Neoclassical style into a compact form that would fit in a fashionable city apartment.

Artists and designers in the United States made especially literal references to the modern age by incorporating images of machine technology and urban life. Futurist painter Joseph Stella, for example, composed several paintings of New York's Brooklyn Bridge, completed in 1883, which was hailed as an engineering wonder and a symbol of the great achievements of the modern city (fig. 30). In the decorative arts, designers used forms suggestive of skyscrapers, electricity, high-speed trains, and modern machinery in everything from furniture to cocktail shakers. Viktor Schreckengost's punch bowl playfully celebrated New York's nightlife, complete with dancing girls and bottles of champagne (p. 184–185). Both Stella and Schreckengost expressed in their work the syncopated rhythms of jazz music, the angular geometry of the cityscape, and the patterns of light and shadow cast by blazing electric lights.

Perhaps the most significant development in the realm of decorative arts in this period was the rise of the industrial designer. In the 1920s and 1930s, when professionalization and scientific efficiency became dominant cultural values, industrial designers worked to make products appealing to the consumer and therefore profitable for the manufacturer; some designers, like Russel Wright, became household names. As in sculpture and painting, many influential figures in the field were European emigrants, including Paul Frankl, Walter von Nessen, and Kem Weber. American-born designers like Walter Dorwin Teague were heavily influenced by European modernist design theories espoused by Le Corbusier and Walter Gropius.

In the 1940s and 1950s, the role of the designer took on new meaning as the doctrine of functionalism and "good design" became the prevailing aesthetic standard. Heavily promoted by the Museum of Modern Art in New York through numerous design exhibitions, good design was intended to ensure not only manufacturer's profits but also lasting moral and aesthetic quality in the material objects of everyday life. The idea was rooted in a belief that objects could be judged by such universal standards as suitability to function, "honesty" of construction, and "truth" to materials. While this moral idealism harked back to

fig. 29. (previous page) **Length of furnishing fabric, Du Pont Rayon Company, design attributed to Thomas Lamb (1896–1988), New York, New York, about 1930.**

Ruskin and the Arts and Crafts Movement, good-design theory also celebrated capitalism and the democratizing power of machine-age technology.

The objects designed by Charles and Ray Eames in the 1940s have become familiar icons of good design, so much so that it is easy to overlook how innovative they were in their own day. Their designs, including molded plywood and plastic chairs, were among the first mass-produced goods to make use of materials and technologies developed for military purposes during World War II, and their durability and low cost made them ubiquitous in commercial and institutional settings. Their successful blend of comfort and clean-lined aesthetics helped make modernism accessible to a mass audience. At the same time, links between industry and handcraft were not entirely severed; some craftspeople, including John Prip, worked simultaneously in the worlds of industrial design and studio craft.

fig. 30. **Joseph Stella** (1877–1946), *Old Brooklyn Bridge*, New York, New York, about 1940.

American sculptors in the first half of the twentieth century, including European emigrant artists and Americans working abroad, responded to the machine age by separating their craft from mass-produced modernist design and emphasizing unique individual expression. Sculptors challenged the prevailing mode of academic classical sculpture, in which the artist produced a clay model which was then replicated in marble or bronze by skilled assistants and technicians. Viewing this process as overly mechanical, they turned to the radically different technique of direct carving in stone or wood. Direct carving became an international phenomenon, pioneered by New York-based French emigrant Robert Laurent, which allowed the artist to create the sculpture from start to finish in his own studio and encouraged spontaneity in the execution of the work.

Along with this new emphasis on the sculptor's direct engagement with materials, other artists rethought the role and purpose of modern sculpture. In the nineteenth century, sculpture was generally valued as commemorative and morally inspiring public art, but early twentieth-century sculptors like Alexander Calder began to regard their work as a vehicle for individualistic expression of emotions or formal relationships. Sculptural realism and public commemorative sculpture persisted as well, but with a modern sensibility. In his emotionally powerful *Pennsylvania Railroad War Memorial*, Walker Hancock stylized and streamlined the figures of the dying soldier and angel to deemphasize their individuality and make them appear as universal symbols of suffering and redemption.

Resting Stag

Elie Nadelman (1882–1946)
New York, New York, about 1916–17
Bronze, original onyx base

A native of Warsaw who studied classical art in Munich and moved to Paris in 1904, Elie Nadelman was immersed in the world of the European avant-garde. As he worked to develop his own distinctive style, Nadelman drew upon the smooth linearity and restrained expression of classical Greek art to create boldly simplified figures with curving lines. His work achieved critical acclaim during his years in Paris and attracted the attention of an American patron, Helena Rubenstein. In August 1914, at the outbreak of World War I, Rubenstein helped Nadelman relocate to New York.

Resting Stag is one of a group of animal figures Nadelman created in preparation for an exhibition at the New York gallery Scott and Fowles in 1917.

A stylized and graceful work, its clean, flowing lines reflect Nadelman's synthesis of classical ideals and modern influences. The streamlined contours and luxurious surfaces of the bronze figure and onyx base foreshadowed the sophisticated Art Deco look that emerged in the 1920s.

H. 45.7 cm, w. 53.3 cm, d. including base 26.7 cm
(H. 18 in., w. 21 in., d. including base 10½ in.)
Museum purchase with funds donated by Frank B. Bemis Fund, Barbara L. and Theodore B. Alfond, an anonymous donor, Edwin E. Jack Fund, Arthur Mason Knapp Fund, Ernest Kahn Fund, Arthur Tracy Cabot Fund, Frederick Brown Fund, Morris and Louise Rosenthal Fund, Samuel Putnam Avery Fund, and Joyce Arnold Rusoff Fund 2002.1
Reproduced by permission of the estate of Elie Nadelman.

Armoire

**The Company of Master Craftsmen
for W. & J. Sloane (1925–1942)**
Flushing, New York, 1925–35
Mahogany, lumber-core plywood, cherry,
tulipwood, maple, rosewood, brass

In the early 1920s, many Americans, including critics, journalists, and even government officials believed that there was little or no good modern design being produced in the United States. In response to that concern, several of the nation's leading museums and department stores sought to instruct and inspire designers and improve consumer's taste by exposing them to good styles of the past and the exciting new fashions coming from Europe. In 1925, for example, New York's top furniture retailer, W. & J. Sloane, established a manufacturing subsidiary named the Company of Master Craftsmen to create affordable reproductions of antiques from a "golden age" of furniture design. Sloane collaborated with curators at the Metropolitan Museum of Art to make exact copies of some of the museum's furniture, calling its products "registered reproductions" and suggesting that their faithful reiteration of accepted masterpieces from the past would elevate current taste.

At the same time, the Metropolitan Museum showcased the latest Art Deco designs in a touring exhibition of modern furniture by French designer Jacques-Emile Ruhlmann. The Company of Master Craftsmen quickly added this new, alternative source for improving the sophistication of American furniture to their repertoire. They developed adaptations of the French designs, such as this armoire, part of an en suite bedroom set. In name, form, and ornament, this piece emulates Ruhlmann's furniture. Yet its innovative and less expensive materials and construction techniques,

including the use of a sprayed-on finish of newly invented cellulose nitrate lacquer as a shiny, protective top coat, demonstrate American ingenuity.

H. 134.6 cm, w. 92.7 cm, d. 52.1 cm
(H. 53 in., w. 36½ in., d. 20½ in.)
Gift of Priscilla Cunningham in honor of Charles C. Cunningham, Jr., and Thomas L. Cunningham 2004.2200

Punch bowl from the Jazz Bowl series

Cowan Pottery Studio (active 1919–1931); designed by
Viktor Schreckengost (born 1906)
Rocky River, Ohio, 1931
Glazed porcelain with sgraffito decoration

Requesting something "New Yorkish," Eleanor Roosevelt commissioned a punch bowl in 1931 for her husband, Franklin D. Roosevelt, then governor of New York. Twenty-six-year-old designer Viktor Schreckengost created a bowl inspired by the New Year's Eve festivities he had recently enjoyed in the city. The motifs on the bowl recalled his memories of the brilliant artificial lighting of Broadway and Times Square, jazz music and Radio City Music Hall, illegal cocktails sipped in nightclubs, and the starry night sky glimpsed above looming skyscrapers. The bowl's linear design, the playful irregularity of the sgraffito (incised) decoration, and the bold blue and black colors reflected the influence of modern Viennese graphic design and ceramics.

Mrs. Roosevelt was so pleased with the bowl that she immediately ordered two more, confident that they would be useful after her husband was elected president in 1932. After the design received much acclaim, Cowan Pottery produced a small series of similar bowls, including this one. Manufacture could not keep up with demand, however, because the bowl's sgraffito decoration had to be done by hand. Although Schreckengost refined the design twice to make the process faster and cheaper, production was still too time consuming and the series was discontinued. Dubbed the Jazz Bowl series (after the word *JAZZ* in the design), the bowls capture the nervous energy of urban nightlife and have become regarded as icons of American Art Deco.

H. 22.9 cm, diam. base 19.1 cm, diam. rim 42.9 cm
(H. 9 in., diam. base 7½ in., diam. rim 16⅞ in.)
Gift of John P. Axelrod   1990.507

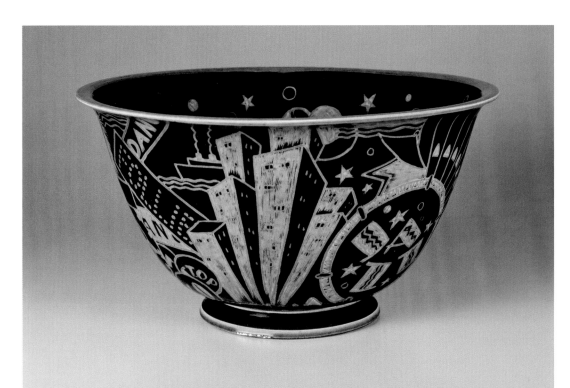

Diana

Alexander Calder (1898–1976)

Probably New York, New York, about 1934

Walnut, steel pins, iron base

Although more widely known for his mobiles and wire sculptures, Alexander Calder, a third-generation sculptor, made art in many media. In his early career he made more than fifty wood sculptures reflecting the influence of the direct-carving method that such avant-garde sculptors as José de Creeft, Chaim Gross, and William Zorach were exhibiting widely. These artists eschewed traditional methods for making fine sculpture, in which the sculptor's original plaster model was reproduced in marble or bronze by other artisans. They preferred direct, personal engagement with the material—either wood or stone—to carve stylized figures inspired by the spare forms of American folk art, including bird decoys and weather vanes.

Calder began making wood sculptures in the late 1920s, about the same time he started creating figurative wire sculptures. In his earliest carvings, usually animals or female figures, he allowed the distinctive grain or shape of the wood to suggest the final form; he resisted the suggestion that he produce multiple versions of his 1928 Cow sculpture, explaining, "That piece of wood turned out to be a cow, but the next one might be a cat. How do I know?" As Calder's other works became increasingly abstract in the mid-1930s, so did his wood sculptures. Diana reflects this later phase in its smooth, streamlined shapes that subtly suggest a female figure crowned by a crescent moon. Rather than being carved from a single block of wood, Diana is a "stabile" sculpture assembled from component parts that do not move but that suggest a tenuous sense of balance.

H. 77.5 cm, w. 45.1 cm, d. 48.9 cm
(H. 30½ in., w. 17¾ in., d. 19¼ in.)
Frederick Brown Fund 60.956

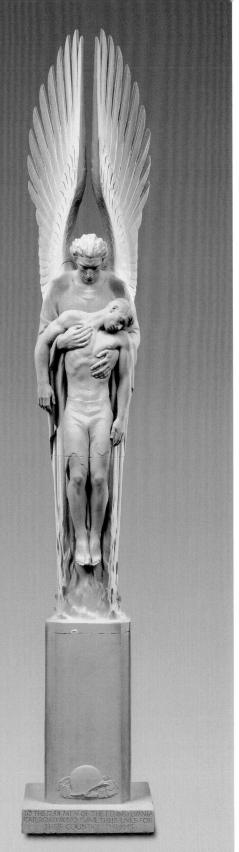

Scale model for *Pennsylvania Railroad War Memorial*

Walker Hancock (1901–1998)

Lanesville, Massachusetts, 1949–52

Painted plaster with mixed media armature

Walker Hancock, dean of American figurative sculptors in the twentieth century, is perhaps best known for his *Pennsylvania Railroad War Memorial.* Weighing ten-and-a-half tons and standing about forty feet tall, this bronze sculpture of an enormous winged angel lifting a dying soldier was commissioned for the grand concourse of Thirtieth Street station in Philadelphia. Dedicated in 1952, it commemorates the ultimate sacrifice made by more than thirteen hundred men and women of the Pennsylvania Railroad during World War II.

As Hancock explained, "the tall vertical form" of the monument was dictated by the architecture of the cavernous space it was designed to occupy; the sculpture blends harmoniously with the fluted columns and windows of the station. Avoiding sentimentality, Hancock fashioned the figures in his own manner of modern classical realism, featuring broad surfaces and simple yet powerful forms. The plaster model of the memorial seen here, about one-third the size of the completed work, remained in the artist's studio on Cape Ann, Massachusetts, until his death.

Born in Saint Louis, Hancock studied at the American Academy in Rome in the 1920s and spent much of his professional life as a professor at the Pennsylvania Academy of the Fine Arts in Philadelphia, where he had been a student of the famous portrait sculptor Charles Grafly. During his long career, he created a large body of architectural sculpture, war memorials, religious works, portraits (including many figure studies of presidents), and medals. While he achieved widespread acclaim as a key figure in modern realism, Hancock was known as much for his strength of character and noble spirit as for the high quality of his work.

H. approximately 365.8 cm (144 in.)
Bequest of Walker Hancock   2002.377

DCM (Dining Chair Metal)

Evans Products Company; distributed by Herman
Miller Manufacturing Company (1923–present),
Zeeland, Michigan; designed by Charles Eames
(1907–1978)
Venice, California, designed and made in 1946–47
Ash plywood, steel tubing, rubber shock mounts
H. 74.6 cm, w. 48.9 cm, d. 50.8 cm (H. 29⅜ in., w. 19¼ in., d. 20 in.)
Gift of Edward J. Wormley 1975.31

DCW (Dining Chair Wood)

Evans Products Company; distributed by Herman
Miller Manufacturing Company (1923–present),
Zeeland, Michigan; designed by Charles Eames
(1907–1978)
Venice, California, designed and made in 1946–47
Plywood with walnut veneer
H. 73.3 cm, w. 48.9 cm, d. 52.1 cm
(H. 28⅞ in., w. 19¼ in., d. 20½ in.)
Gift of Edward J. Wormley 1975.32

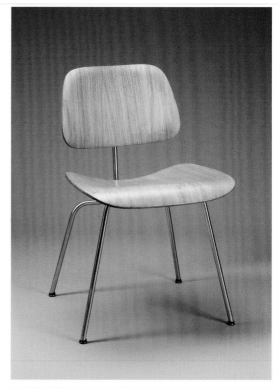

RAR (Rocking Armchair Rod)

Herman Miller Manufacturing Company
(1923–present); molded by Zenith Plastics Company,
Gardena, California; designed by Charles Eames
(1907–1978) and Ray Eames (1912–1989)
Zeeland, Michigan, designed about 1948–50,
made about 1950–53
Molded polyester fiberglass composite, steel and
birch rockers, rubber shock mounts
H. 68.9 cm, w. 62.9 cm, d. 59.7 cm (H. 27 in., w. 24¾ in., d. 23½ in.)
Gift of Edward J. Wormley 1975.33

DKR-2 (Dining Bikini Rod)

Herman Miller Manufacturing Company
(1923–present); designed by Charles Eames
(1907–1978)
Zeeland, Michigan, designed 1951, made 1953
Painted steel wire, leather
H. 81.3 cm, w. 44.5 cm, d. 49.5 cm (H. 32 in., w. 17½ in., d. 19½ in.)
Gift of Roger and Doris Goodrich 1985.185

In the early 1940s, designers and newlyweds Charles and Ray Eames pioneered a production method to simultaneously bend plywood in more than one direction, using their homemade Kazam machine. With this innovation, which the artists named for its speed and efficiency—you put in a piece of wood and "Kazam!" It's bent!—they won a commission from the U.S. Navy to design plywood leg splints and stretchers for wounded sailors, featuring compound curves to support the body. They applied the same technology after the war in the body-conforming design of the *DCW* and *DCM.* The two chairs illustrated here were exhibited in 1947 at the Museum of Modern Art, after which the Eameses gave them to their friend and fellow furniture designer Edward J. Wormley. These early examples show details of the original design—such as the rubber caps on the feet—that were modified in later production.

With the *RAR* and *DKR-2,* the Eameses continued their efforts to design comfortable and affordable furniture using new industrial materials. They originally designed the *RAR* to be shaped in metal and sprayed with a neoprene coating (a synthetic rubber) for comfort. However, by the time the chair went into production in 1950, the manufacturer, Herman Miller Furniture, was able to make the seat in polyester, reinforced with strands of fiberglass and easily molded into an enveloping bucket shape. Customers could order the lightweight plastic chair in a range of bright, cheerful colors and with a variety of leg options in tubular steel or bent wire. This *DKR-2* chair, with its original blue leather upholstery, is one of a pair donated to the Museum by the owners of a prototype house with modern furnishings that was featured in a 1954 issue of *Better Homes and Gardens,* a leading disseminator of home fashion. These four chairs represent the convergence of modern design with innovative technology, mass manufacturing and marketing, and popular consumer taste in the postwar era.

Contour beverage service

Towle Manufacturing Company (established 1882); designed by Robert J. King (born 1917) with John Van Koert (1912–1998), director of design

Newburyport, Massachusetts, 1953–about 1960

Silver, melamine

Pitcher: H. 26 cm, w. 17.8 cm, diam. base 8.4 cm, wt. 705.9 gm (H. 10¼ in., w. 7 in., diam. base 3⁹⁄₁₆ in., wt. 22 oz. 13 dwt. 21 gr.)

Museum purchase with funds provided by The Seminarians in memory of Nathaniel T. Dexter   2001.260.1–3

Onion teapot

John Prip (born 1922)

Rochester, New York, 1954

Silver, ebony, rattan

H. 15.8 cm, w. 27.5 cm, diam. 19.1 cm, diam. base 7.6 cm, wt. 743.4 gm (H. 6³⁄₁₆ in., w. 10¹³⁄₁₆ in., diam. 7½ in., diam. base 3 in., wt. 23 oz. 18 dwt.)

Gift of Stephen and Betty Jane Andrus   1995.137

In the second half of the twentieth century, large silver manufacturers primarily produced hollowware and flatware in patterns evocative of historical styles. Many consumers, perhaps recognizing silver's long-standing role as an emblem of wealth and family, seemed comfortable with tea sets and other objects in traditional modes. The objects illustrated here represent a departure from that attitude by two New England silver companies in the 1950s.

The venerable Towle Manufacturing Company of Newburyport, Massachusetts, with roots dating to the eighteenth century, developed an interest in contemporary design in the late 1940s under the leadership of its president, Charles C. Withers. The *Contour*

line, released first as flatware and later in the hollow-ware forms shown here, represents the company's initial attempt at marketing modernist silver. Designed by Robert J. King under the direction of John Van Koert, *Contour* is distinguished by its sleek surfaces and biomorphic forms.

Reed and Barton of Taunton, Massachusetts, founded in 1827, similarly began to experiment with contemporary forms in the 1950s. James S. Plaut, the first director of the Institute of Contemporary Art in Boston, introduced a Design in Industry department in 1948 that struck a responsive chord with Roger Hallowell, then president of Reed and Barton. Plaut recommended John Prip as a good candidate to advise Reed and Barton on ways to strengthen the relationship between designer-craftsmen and manufacturers. Born and trained as a silversmith in Denmark, Prip had been recruited in 1948 to establish the metals department at the newly founded School for American Craftsmen in upstate New York. Prip's

handcrafted *Onion* teapot, made in 1954, produced a favorable reaction when shown as a prototype to Reed and Barton in 1957. It subsequently became the basis for the company's *Dimension* production line. Prip's fruitful collaboration with Reed and Barton continued until 1970.

The Studio Craft Movement in America: The Late Twentieth Century

Kelly H. L'Ecuyer

Although American material culture of the twentieth century was dominated by goods designed for mass production, the central values and practices of the Arts and Crafts Movement persisted. Interest in handcrafted objects was kept alive in the 1920s and 1930s by a growing fascination with American folk arts and by myriad federal relief agencies and small private groups that sponsored craft programs for social and economic assistance during the Great Depression. After World War II, increasing numbers of furniture makers, woodworkers, metalsmiths, ceramists, glass blowers, and fiber artists—like the reformers in the earlier Arts and Crafts Movement—rejected what they viewed as banal assembly-line production and sought to reunite designer and craftsperson in a small workshop setting, thus developing the studio craft movement.

During these formative years, the heightened professionalism in American crafts was reflected by the creation of a number of regional and national craft organizations and publications. Philanthropist Aileen Osborn Webb founded the American Craftsman's Cooperative Council (now the American Craft Council) in 1939, the New York craft gallery America House in 1940, the magazine *Craft Horizons* (now *American Craft*) in 1941, and the American Craft Museum (now the Museum of Arts and Design) in 1956. These and other new institutions fostered communication and exchange between likeminded craftspeople, who sought personal expression and artistic independence.

The quality and availability of training in craft media changed significantly after World War II. In contrast to preindustrial craftsmen who trained in traditional apprenticeships, studio craft artists after the war pursued many forms of education, including formal academic programs. Education funds available through the GI Bill (the Serviceman's Readjustment Act of 1944) enabled many returning soldiers to attend college and supported craft programs to help war veterans cope with the transition to civilian life. Jeweler and silversmith Mar-

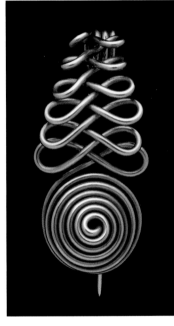

fig. 31. Wirework brooch,

Margret Craver (born 1907),

New York, New York, about 1945.

gret Craver, a nurse during the war, convinced the U.S. surgeon general of the value of metalsmithing as occupational therapy for injured veterans by showing him sample projects that could be accomplished with minimal equipment, such as this wire brooch (fig. 31). With her leadership, the U.S. Army established programs in metalworking at commands and hospitals nationwide. At about the same time, the School for American Craftsmen, founded in 1943 and eventually located at the Rochester Institute of Technology, offered the first four-year college degree in crafts in 1948, and other art schools and colleges added or expanded craft programs in their curricula. Today, hundreds of degree-granting programs in all craft media are available from coast to coast.

Although academic programs gained prominence during the latter half of the twentieth century, many leading studio artists continued to enter the field by unconventional routes. Furniture maker George Nakashima trained as an architect at the Massachusetts Institute of Technology but learned woodworking from a fellow prisoner at an internment camp for Japanese Americans during World War II. He combined these new skills with his design experience and opened his furniture workshop in New Hope, Pennsylvania, after the war. Other studio craftspeople taught themselves their skills through trial-and-error, reading, attending workshops, and communicating with other artists informally or through organizations such as the League of New Hampshire Craftsmen or the Society of North American Goldsmiths. The field continues to attract people with varied backgrounds and self-directed training in the arts and design.

In the last quarter of the twentieth century, an ever-increasing number of exhibitions at museums, galleries, and nonprofit organizations featured craft objects in all media, bringing greater public awareness of the field and helping aspiring craftspeople find models and inspiration for their own work. The Museum of Fine Arts, Boston, began actively collecting twentieth-century studio craft in the 1970s and in 1975 initiated its "Please Be Seated" program, through which studio furniture makers were commissioned to produce gallery seating (fig. 32) for museum visitors. In recent years several museums have been founded or refocused to collect and exhibit studio craft exclusively.

The studio craft movement in America, like the Arts and Crafts Movement at the turn of the twentieth century, has encompassed a wide range of styles, media, artistic influences, and modes of production. Within this diversity, certain generalized chronological trends can be identified. In the 1940s and 1950s, the prevailing dogma of modernist "good design" led to a focus on simple, clean designs; reverence for materials; and functionality in craft objects. While early craft pioneers continued this mode of essentially conservative work through the turbu-

fig. 32. Settee, Wendell Castle (born 1932), Rochester, New York, 1979.

lent years of the 1960s, a new group of "artist-craftsmen," including ceramist Peter Voulkos and furniture maker Tommy Simpson, likened their work to painting and sculpture, abandoned strict ideas about function, used materials in unconventional ways, and infused their work with humor and exuberant self-expression. These efforts provoked tremendous controversy in the field over the nature of "art" versus "craft," a debate many now consider irrelevant but that persists nonetheless.

By the 1970s, the pendulum swung back in favor of skilled technique, and studio craftspeople turned to the explicit display of technical prowess and the exploration of rare, exotic materials. The last two decades of the twentieth century witnessed the growing influence of postmodernism, with its emphasis on personal narrative, historical references, richness of surface ornament, and conceptual rather than purely functional design. Despite these varying trends and the multiplicity of artists in the field, studio crafts are fundamentally unified by the essentially independent nature of the small shops in which they are produced.

Necklace

Art Smith (1917–1982)

New York, New York, about 1958

Sterling silver, semiprecious stones

Art Smith, born in New York to parents of African Caribbean descent, was a seminal figure in the American studio jewelry movement. From 1942 to 1946, Smith studied at the Cooper Union for the Advancement of Science and Art, and during those years he also trained in metalsmithing with jeweler Winifred Mason. Smith later recalled Mason's shop as "a little Bauhaus" and a gathering place for African American artists and writers including Ralph Ellison, Bill Attaway, and Gordon Parks. In 1948, Smith opened his own shop in Greenwich Village, a vibrant art community where many leading modernist jewelers, among them Sam Kramer, Frank Rebajes, and Paul Lobel, had studios within blocks of each other.

Influenced by such prevailing art movements as Constructivism, Surrealism, and Biomorphism, Smith developed an individual style by incorporating in his jewelry the large scale of East African dance regalia, the rhythms of jazz music, and the movement of contemporary African American dance. Designing stage jewelry for the black dance companies led by Talley Beatty, Pearl Primus, and Claude Marchant may have helped Smith develop his sense of theatricality and interest in the relationship of jewelry to the wearer's body. This bold necklace demonstrates his skill in manipulating positive and negative space, creating a sense of flowing movement in asymmetrical, biomorphic forms. As his niece observed, "Arthur . . . had a capacity to deal with all the senses to the fullest. The ears for the music, the eyes for observing beauty, the hands for making it."

H. 43.8 cm, w. 26 cm, d. 1.9 cm (H. 17¼ in., w. 10¼ in., d. ¾ in.)
The Daphne Farago Collection 2006.537

Camelback Mountain

Peter Voulkos (1924–2002)

Probably Berkeley, California, 1959

Stoneware

Peter Voulkos led a group of California ceramists who radically changed American ceramic arts in the 1950s by moving the field toward abstraction, playful handling of materials, and personal expression. Early in the decade, after earning his master of fine arts degree in ceramics at the California College of Arts and Crafts, Voulkos became fascinated by the qualities of improvisation and assemblage found in various media including jazz music, Japanese folk pottery, and the art of Pablo Picasso, Joan Miró, David Smith, and the Abstract Expressionist painters. After founding the ceramics department at the Otis Art Institute in Los Angeles in 1954, he gathered a group of highly talented students who formed something of a revolutionary enclave. His radicalism led to conflict with the institute's director, Millard Sheets, and in 1959 Voulkos left to teach at the University of California, Berkeley. He continued to be an influential teacher for decades, traveling widely and leading exciting workshops during which he demonstrated the spontaneous and playful qualities of his work.

Voulkos assembled *Camelback Mountain* from hollow, wheel-thrown pots, which he then paddled and compressed to destroy their symmetrical shapes. While the clay was still wet, he stacked and attached these altered pots, some gouged or sliced open to reveal internal space, creating a dynamic form with contrasting areas of light and shadow, void and mass. Although the piece exists as a nonfunctional, sculptural object, it also explores the essence of ceramic vessel forms as open and closed containers. Moreover, the work celebrates the earthy and messy qualities of the clay medium. *Camelback Mountain* demonstrates how Voulkos's art revolutionized ceramics, not by merely imitating contemporary sculpture or painting but by exploiting clay in a fresh and direct way.

H. 115.6 cm, w. 49.5 cm, d. 51.4 cm
(H. 45½ in., w. 19½ in., d. 20¼ in.)
Gift of Mr. and Mrs. Stephen D. Paine   1978.690

Rocking chair

Sam Maloof (born in 1916)
Alta Loma, California, 1975
Walnut

The "Maloof rocker" has become the most recognizable and imitated icon of the American studio furniture movement. Admired for its clean curves, graceful proportions, ornamental pinned joints, and rich wood grain, the chair encapsulates the most fully developed qualities of Sam Maloof's work during his nearly sixty-year career.

Maloof is a self-taught woodworker who has been called "a master of the bandsaw" for his skill at freely guiding the saw to create the curved elements of his

seating furniture. Although he uses some templates and produces multiples of similar design, Maloof prides himself on hand shaping each piece. As he has explained, "design does not exist just on paper. It pervades every step in the creation of a piece of furniture." Rather than seeking radical design changes, Maloof makes slight variations and refinements to his basic formula of restrained and functional furniture. The arms of this rocker are gently curved with crisp edges, the sculpted joints make each member of the frame appear to flow into the next, and the seat and backrest are ergonomically shaped to support the sitter in great comfort.

The son of Lebanese immigrants, Maloof worked as a graphic artist and draftsman as a young man and became interested in industrial design after building furniture for his own apartment. He began making furniture full time in 1948 and gained exposure and connections to clients following an important commission from famed industrial designer Henry Dreyfuss. During the 1950s and 1960s, Maloof focused exclusively on commission work and greatly expanded production at his Alta Loma shop to meet a growing demand from West Coast clients. By the 1970s, when he had gained legendary status in the field of American studio furniture and earned numerous prestigious awards, he devoted more time to lectures and workshops.

H. 111.8 cm, w. 70.5 cm, d. 116.9 cm
(H. 44 in., w. 27¾ in., d. 46 in.)
Purchased through funds provided by the National Endowment for the Arts and the Gillette Corporation
1976.122

Delight Rocking Chair

Martha Rising (born in 1954)

Los Angeles, California, 1980

Maple, purpleheart, Andaman padauk

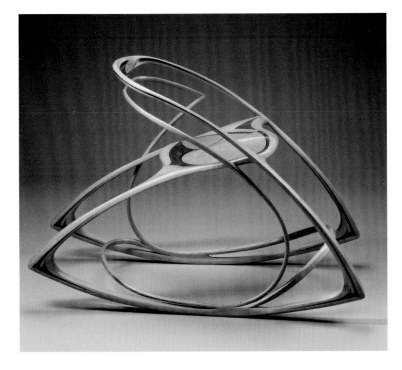

A masterpiece of technical skill and expressive qualities, Martha Rising's bentwood rocking chair uses slender laminated members and curved joinery to suggest dynamic motion. Rising accented the light-colored maple frame with padauk and purpleheart; thin strips of these darker woods function like racing stripes on an automobile to heighten the impression of energy and movement. As Rising explained in 1984, "The dynamic vitality and rhythm I seek to give each piece allows a relationship to the piece beyond its utilitarian function—it portrays a moment of motion captured or portrayed in the piece." Although the chair pushes the boundaries of function, Rising demonstrated a traditionalist's sensitivity to the use of wood as a material. In a 1983 article otherwise disparaging art furniture that was conceptual rather than practical, contemporary furniture maker Art Carpenter praised the care and skill evident in this chair, which he called "a delight of bent forms and fine joinery, a tour de force of craftsmanship which if taken a step further could have become a parody of the bender's art."

Rising (now Martha Rising Rosson) was active in studio furniture making in California from the late 1970s through the mid-1980s. Like other second-generation studio furniture makers, her training included both informal and academic education. After learning basic woodworking and design methods from her father in his home workshop, she majored in "design in wood" in the art department at California State University, Northridge. There she earned a bachelor's and a master's degree in fine arts; visited Carpenter's studios and those of two other noted California furniture makers, Sam Maloof and Larry Hunter; and apprenticed with wood sculptor Michael Jean Cooper. Cooper's use of complex three-dimensional bending and exotic woods in various colors strongly influenced Rising's work, although unlike Cooper, Rising consciously strove to remain, in her words, within "the vocabulary of . . . utilitarian furniture."

H. 85.1 cm, w. 60.3 cm, d. 125.8 cm

(H. 33½ in., w. 23¾ in., d. 49½ in.)

Gift of the artist, Martha Rising Rosson 2004.256

Clock

Frank E. Cummings III (born in 1938)

Long Beach, California, 1979–80

Ebony, ivory, African blackwood, 14k gold, black star sapphires, glass

This tall-case clock by Frank E. Cummings III represents the height of technical virtuosity that emerged in the field of studio furniture in the 1970s. While other artisans at that time were also intrigued by the challenge of building handmade wooden clockworks, Cummings took the art to a new level by using rare precious materials and an idiosyncratic design. This clock's ebony and ivory frame is enclosed with three curved glass panels to reveal its intricate works, including gears delicately hand carved in ivory and African blackwood and pinions mounted with black star sapphires set in gold. Nearly a year in the making, the clock is perhaps the ultimate "super-object," reflecting the period's emphasis on technical prowess and exotic materials.

Cummings designed and built the clock intuitively, having no training in clock making. He learned some rudimentary principles of gear mechanics by examining nineteenth-century wooden clocks owned by a local clock repairer, but created his own elaborate calculations and drawings for his clockworks. He manipulated the materials with great deliberation; the African blackwood used in the gears was chosen for its extreme hardness and durability, and the grain of the wood and the grain of the ivory in the gears were set in opposite directions to prevent warping. An admirer of the inventive experimentation of Leonardo da Vinci, Cummings took pride in developing his own way of making a functional clock.

Cummings teaches at California State University, Fullerton. He makes furniture and turned vessels with a variety of precious materials, emphasizing time-intensive workmanship. Inspired by the spiritual meanings of everyday objects in Africa, where he has also studied and taught, and by the religious

significance of simple, well-made Shaker furniture, Cummings seeks to reinvest meaning and beauty in functional objects.

H. 172.7 cm, w. 61 cm, d. 40.6 cm (H. 68 in., w. 24 in., d. 16 in.)
Museum purchase with funds donated anonymously and from a Gift of The Seminarians in memory of William A. Whittemore and Beck F. Whittemore, and with funds donated by Anne M. Beha and Robert A. Radloff, Susan W. Paine, The Doran Family Charitable Trust, and by exchange from a Gift of J. Templeman Coolidge, Gift of Miss Ruth K. Richardson, Gift of Richard S. Fuller in memory of his wife, Lucy Derby Fuller, Gift of Miss Annie J. Pecker, Gift of William E. Beaman, Gift of George R. Meneely, Gift of Joseph Randolph Coolidge IV, Bequest of Mrs. Ethel Stanwood Bolton, Bequest of Dr. Samuel A. Green, Bequest of Miss Eleanor P. Martin, Bequest of Miss Kate A. Gould, and Bequest of Sarah E. Montague   2004.563

Standing cup with cover

Richard Mawdsley (born in 1945)

Carterville, Illinois, 1986

Silver

Richard Mawdsley's standing cup with cover combines a traditional form with his distinctive, mechanically inspired embellishment to create a masterpiece of contemporary hollowware. As in his jewelry of the 1970s and 1980s, the intricate ornament is composed of commercial metal tubing of various sizes shaped and manipulated to create a rich composition centering on an expertly fashioned human figure. Unlike his necklaces with similar decoration, however, the form of this cup evokes a sense of sacred ritual through its reference to traditional communion vessels. The ornament on the stem thus puts both mechanical imagery and the human figure in a spiritual and liturgical context.

Mawdsley's interest in machine imagery began in the 1960s during his undergraduate studies in metals at Kansas State Teacher's College, where he made Pop Art–inspired castings of industrial cogs and gears. As a graduate student at the University of Kansas, Lawrence, he was influenced by the whimsical metal toys of Brent Kington and the technical finesse of master goldsmith John Paul Miller. By 1970, Mawdsley developed what he has called the "one good basic idea" that has driven his work for three decades: the use of metal tubing for both structure and ornament. Exploring variations on this theme has not limited the range of forms he produces. In fact, Mawdsley is one of only a handful of metalsmiths to create silver hollowware (in addition to jewelry) in recent years, making this remarkable cup an unusual and important example of twentieth-century studio metalwork.

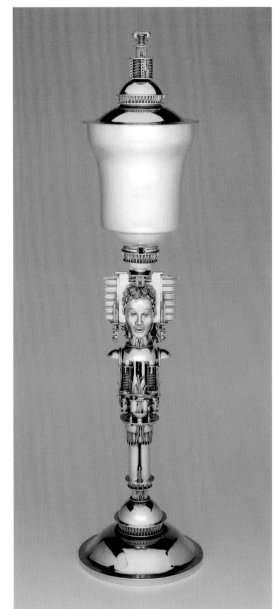

H. 43.8 cm, diam. rim 9.2 cm, diam. foot 9.2 cm,
wt. 817.1 gm (H. 17³/₁₆ in., diam. rim 3⁵/₈ in.,
diam. foot 3⁵/₈ in., wt. 26 oz. 5 dwt. 10 gr.)
Anonymous gift   1988.535a–b

Leopard Chest

Judy Kensley McKie (born in 1944)

Cambridge, Massachusetts, 1989

Basswood with oil paint and gold leaf

After earning a degree in painting at the Rhode Island School of Design, Judy McKie turned to furniture making in the early 1970s. Her first designs were utilitarian, but as she gained proficiency she desired greater personal expression. Seeking to make "inanimate objects that are animated," McKie looked to the art of Precolumbian, African, and Native American cultures for inspiration. She developed her own vocabulary of abstracted plants and animals to enliven her works, either as surface decoration or as sculpted structural members.

The stylized, grinning leopards that decorate all sides of this chest represent the best qualities of McKie's imaginative and expressive carved furniture. McKie created this chest in response to a painted, carved, and gilded one in the MFA's collection by Charles Prendergast (see below). She shares Prendergast's interest in using surface decoration to evoke a sense of "primitivism" and mystery. To ornament the *Leopard Chest,* McKie carved and painted the basswood panels, and built up a japanned surface using layers of shellac and boule (a red pigment). She painted the chest and rubbed the frame with cotton to create an aged finish, and then gold leafed, burnished, and rubbed the carved leopards. The result is a richly varied surface that is both elegant and energetic.

McKie uses efficient joinery and plain-figured woods so as not to distract from her designs, and sometimes (as here) she hires other craftsmen to

fig. 33. **Chest, Charles James Prendergast** (1863–1948), New York, New York, and Westport, Connecticut, 1926–27.

execute the basic case construction. Simplifying the construction process allows her to focus on visual expression through her carving and finishes. She has explained, "I think first of the image. The craftsmanship is very much integrated in the work, but I don't think it is more important than the idea."

H. 84.8 cm, w. 126.7 cm, d. 45.7 cm
(H. 33⅜ in., w. 49⅞ in., d. 18 in.)
Anonymous gift 1991.444

Mirage Lake

Wayne Higby (born in 1943)

Alfred, New York, 1984

Raku-fired earthenware

Wayne Higby studied painting in college but became a ceramist after an epiphany during a junior-year trip abroad. While traveling in the Mediterranean, he visited the Heraklion Museum on the island of Crete, where he encountered Minoan pots of the Bronze Age. As he later described the experience, he was swept away by the pots and their "magnificent sense of shape, volume," and painted decoration; he claims, "I became a potter the day I walked into that museum." Upon his return to the United States, Higby sought out training in ceramics and studied with studio potters Betty Woodman and Fred Bauer. He has since become a leader in American ceramics, teaching for more than thirty years at the famed New York State College of Ceramics in Alfred, New York, and producing work that has been exhibited and acquired by major museums across the country.

A landscape image that envelops both the interior and exterior of a vessel is the dominant motif of Higby's elegant ceramics. The artist credits his childhood in Colorado with instilling his love of "being in the landscape." Like the nineteenth-century American landscape painters he admires, including Albert Bierstadt and Frederick Edwin Church, Higby says he tries to capture a sense of being in a particular geographic place. At the same time, he highly values the clay vessel as a format for his work, focusing particularly on the large bowl form because of its universal, abstract qualities.

H. 28.3 cm, diam. rim 47 cm, diam. base 14.6 cm
(H. 11⅛ in., diam. rim 18½ in., diam. base 5¾ in.)
Gift of Mary-Louise Meyer in Memory of Norman Meyer
1984.770

Soleggiata Serena

Toots Zynsky (born in 1951)

Providence, Rhode Island, 2000

Filet-de-verre glass (fused and thermo-formed colored glass threads)

Toots Zynsky's distinct contribution to the studio glass movement is her original method of fusing and shaping layers of fine glass threads into vessel forms. Using thousands of hair-thin threads of varying colors and lengths, Zynsky places groups of them together in patches of color on a board, so that the bottom layer will eventually form the outside of the vessel. She then heats the flat layers of threads until they fuse, removing the layered glass from the oven at varying stages to manipulate it into a bowl form with spatulas or to slump (or bend) it in a steel bowl or mold. The threads remain distinct after fusing, so that the vessel appears to be made of many delicate fibers; the overlapping streaks of color resemble a painter's brushstrokes. Deeply fluted edges allow the viewer to consider the inner and outer surfaces of this bowl simultaneously.

Zynsky trained during the early years of the studio glass movement, when a great sense of experimenta-tion prevailed. She studied with famed glass artist Dale Chihuly at the Rhode Island School of Design in the early 1970s and was later one of the first students at his Pilchuck Glass School in Seattle. After working in multimedia art, she developed her technique of fus-ing hand-pulled glass threads in the mid-1980s while living in Amsterdam. Mathijs Tenission Van Manen, a Dutch inventor who visited her studio in 1982, built a machine allowing her to pull the threads in a fraction of the time the process had formerly required. As Zyn-sky has explained, glass is "amazing" because "you can do everything with it. You can pour it and cast it like metal. You can stretch it, carve it, saw it, you can stick it together . . . It's such a strange and plastic thing. I think that's what keeps drawing me back to it."

H. 27.9 cm, w. 62.9 cm, d. 22.9 cm (H. 11 in., w. 24¾ in., d. 9 in.)
Gift of the artist in honor of Evelyn and John Zynsky
2001.281

Suggestions for Further Reading

American Decorative Arts and Sculpture in the Museum of Fine Arts, Boston

Buhler, Kathryn C. *American Silver, 1655–1825, in the Museum of Fine Arts, Boston.* 2 vols. Boston: Museum of Fine Arts, 1972.

Fairbanks, Jonathan. "A Decade of Collecting Decorative Arts and Sculpture at the Museum of Fine Arts, Boston." *Antiques* 120, no. 3 (September 1981): 590–636.

Fairbanks, Jonathan L., et al. *American Pewter in the Museum of Fine Arts, Boston.* Boston: Museum of Fine Arts, 1974.

Fairbanks, Jonathan L., et al. *Collecting American Decorative Arts and Sculpture, 1971–1991.* Boston: Museum of Fine Arts, 1991.

Fairbanks, Jonathan L., et al. Special issue on the Oak Hill period rooms, *Museum of Fine Arts, Boston, Bulletin* 81 (1983).

Greenthal, Kathryn, Paula M. Kozol, and Jan Seidler Ramirez, with an introduction by Jonathan L. Fairbanks. *American Figurative Sculpture in the Museum of Fine Arts, Boston.* Boston: Museum of Fine Arts, 1986.

Hipkiss, Edwin J. *Eighteenth-Century American Arts: The M. and M. Karolik Collection.* Cambridge, MA: Harvard University Press in association with the Museum of Fine Arts, Boston, 1941.

Hipkiss, Edwin J. *Handbook of the Department of Decorative Arts of Europe and America.* Boston: Museum of Fine Arts, 1928.

Hipkiss, Edwin J. *The Philip Leffingwell Spalding Collection of Early American Silver.* Cambridge, MA: Harvard University Press in association with the Museum of Fine Arts, Boston, 1943.

Hipkiss, Edwin J. *Three McIntire Rooms from Peabody, Massachusetts.* Boston: Museum of Fine Arts, 1931.

Randall, Richard H., Jr. *American Furniture in the Museum of Fine Arts, Boston.* Boston: Museum of Fine Arts, 1965.

Stebbins, Theodore S., Carol Troyen, and Gerald W. R. Ward. *A Significant Story: Treasures of American Painting and Decorative Arts from the M. and M. Karolik Collections of the Museum of Fine Arts, Boston.* Newport, RI: Newport Art Museum, 1993.

Ward, Gerald W. R., et al. *American Folk: Folk Art from the Collection of the Museum of Fine Arts, Boston.* Boston: Museum of Fine Arts, 2001.

General Works

American Furniture. Milwaukee, WI: Chipstone Foundation, 1993–. Distributed by University Press of New England, Hanover, NH. Annual periodical.

Ames, Kenneth L., and Gerald W. R. Ward, eds. *Decorative Arts and Household Furnishings in America, 1650–1920: An Annotated Bibliography.* Winterthur, DE: Winterthur Museum, 1989. Distributed by University Press of Virginia, Charlottesville.

Bishop, Robert, and Patricia Coblentz. *American Decorative Arts: Three Hundred Sixty Years of Creative Design.* New York: Harry N. Abrams, 1982.

Ceramics in America. Milwaukee, WI: Chipstone Foundation, 2001–. Distributed by University Press of New England, Hanover, NH. Annual periodical.

Cooke, Edward S., Jr., ed. *Upholstery in America and Europe: From the Seventeenth Century to World War I.* New York and London: W. W. Norton, 1987. A Barra Foundation Book.

Cooper, Wendy A. *In Praise of America: American Decorative Arts, 1650–1830; Fifty Years of Discovery since the 1929 Girl Scouts Loan Exhibition.* New York: Alfred A. Knopf, 1980.

Craven, Wayne. *Sculpture in America.* New York: Thomas Y. Crowell, 1968.

Fairbanks, Jonathan L., and Elizabeth Bidwell Bates. *American Furniture, 1620 to the Present.* New York: Richard Marek Publishers, 1981.

Fennimore, Donald L. *Iron at Winterthur.* Winterthur, DE: Henry Francis du Pont Winterthur Museum, 2004. Distributed by University Press of New England, Hanover, NH.

Spectral-Luma Ellipse 2000, Tom Patti (born 1943), Pittsfield, Massachusetts, 2000.

Fennimore, Donald L. *Metalwork in Early America: Copper and Its Alloys from the Winterthur Collection*. Winterthur, DE: Henry Francis du Pont Winterthur Museum, 1996. Distributed by Antique Collectors' Club.

Fitzgerald, Oscar P. *Four Centuries of American Furniture*. Radnor, PA: Wallace-Homestead, 1995.

Frelinghuysen, Alice Cooney. *American Porcelain, 1770–1920*. New York: Metropolitan Museum of Art, 1989. Distributed by Harry N. Abrams, New York.

Kirk, John T. *American Furniture: Understanding Style, Construction, and Quality*. New York: Harry N. Abrams, 2000.

Krill, Rosemary Troy, with Pauline K. Eversmann. *Early American Decorative Arts, 1620–1820: A Handbook for Interpreters*. Walnut Creek, CA: AltaMira Press, 2001.

Mayhew, Edgar de Noailles, and Minor Myers, Jr. *A Documentary History of American Interiors: From the Colonial Era to 1915*. New York: Charles Scribner's Sons, 1980.

McKearin, George S., and Helen McKearin. *American Glass*. New York: Bonanza, 1950.

Metropolitan Museum of Art. *Mexico: Splendors of Thirty Centuries*. New York: Metropolitan Museum of Art; Boston: Little, Brown, Bulfinch Press, 1990.

Montgomery, Charles F. *A History of American Pewter*. Rev. ed. New York: Dutton, 1978.

Phipps, Elena, et al. *The Colonial Andes: Tapestries and Silverwork, 1530–1830*. New York: Metropolitan Museum of Art, 2004.

Priddy, Sumpter. *American Fancy: Exuberance in the Arts, 1790–1840*. Milwaukee, WI: Chipstone Foundation, 2004.

Puig, Francis J., and Michael Conforti, eds. *The American Craftsman and the European Tradition, 1620–1820*. Minneapolis: Minneapolis Institute of Arts, 1989. Distributed by University Press of New England, Hanover, NH.

Tolles, Thayer, ed. *American Sculpture in the Metropolitan Museum of Art*. 2 vols. New York: Metropolitan Museum of Art, 1999–2001.

Ward, Barbara McLean, and Gerald W. R. Ward, eds. *Silver in American Life*. New York: American Federation of Arts; Boston: David R. Godine, 1979.

The Arts of New England in the Seventeenth and Early Eighteenth Centuries

Baarsen, Reinier, and Cooper-Hewitt Museum. *Courts and Colonies: The William and Mary Style in Holland, England, and America*. New York: Cooper-Hewitt Museum, 1988.

Fairbanks, Jonathan L., and Robert F. Trent. *New England Begins: The Seventeenth Century*. 3 vols. Boston: Museum of Fine Arts, 1982.

Forman, Benno M. *American Seating Furniture, 1630–1730: An Interpretive Catalogue*. New York: W. W. Norton, 1988. A Winterthur Book.

Kane, Patricia E., ed. *Colonial Massachusetts Silversmiths and Jewelers*. New Haven, CT: Yale University Art Gallery, 1998. Distributed by University Press of New England, Hanover, NH.

Trent, Robert F., ed. *Pilgrim Century Furniture: An Historical Survey*. New York: Main Street Press / Universe Books, 1976.

Arts of the Colonial Americas: The Eighteenth Century

Bowman, Leslie Greene, and Morrison H. Heckscher. *American Rococo, 1750–1775: Elegance in Ornament*. Los Angeles: Los Angeles County Museum of Art; New York: Metropolitan Museum of Art, 1992. Distributed by Harry N. Abrams.

Fairbanks, Jonathan L., et al. *Paul Revere's Boston, 1735–1818*. Boston: Museum of Fine Arts, 1975.

Fales, Martha Gandy. *Early American Silver*. 2nd. ed. New York: E. P. Dutton, 1973.

Fane, Diana, ed. *Converging Cultures: Art and Identity in Spanish America*. New York: Harry N. Abrams, 1996.

Jobe, Brock, and Myrna Kaye, with the assistance of Philip Zea. *New England Furniture, the Colonial Era: Selections from the Society for the Preservation of New England Antiquities*. Boston: Houghton Mifflin, 1984.

Kirk, John T. *American Furniture and the British Tradition to 1830*. New York: Alfred A. Knopf, 1982.

Mo, Charles L. *Splendors of the New World: Spanish Colonial Masterworks from the Viceroyalty of Peru*. Charlotte, NC: Mint Museum of Art, 1992.

Palmer, Arlene. *Glass in Early America: Selections from the Henry Francis du Pont Winterthur Museum*. Winterthur, DE: Henry Francis du Pont Winterthur Museum, 1993.

Whitehill, Walter Muir, Brock Jobe, and Jonathan L. Fairbanks, eds. *Boston Furniture of the Eighteenth Century*. Boston: Colonial Society of Massachusetts, 1974. Distributed by University Press of Virginia, Charlottesville.

Neoclassicism and the New Nation: The Late Eighteenth and Early Nineteenth Centuries

Cooper, Wendy A. *Classical Taste in America, 1800–1840*. New York: Abbeville Press / Baltimore Museum of Art, 1993.

Montgomery, Charles F. *American Furniture: The Federal Period in the Henry Francis du Pont Winterthur Museum*. New York: Viking Press, 1966. A Winterthur Book.

Mussey, Robert D., Jr. *The Furniture Masterworks of John and Thomas Seymour*. Salem, MA: Peabody Essex Museum, 2003. Distributed by University Press of New England, Hanover, NH.

American Diversity: Folk Traditions and Vernacular Expressions

Ames, Kenneth L. *Beyond Necessity: Art in the Folk Tradition*. Winterthur, DE: Winterthur Museum, 1977. Distributed by W. W. Norton, New York.

Glassie, Henry H. *Material Culture*. Bloomington: Indiana University Press, 1999.

Koverman, Jill Beute, ed. *I Made This Jar: The Life and Works of the Enslaved African-American Potter, Dave*. Columbia, SC: McKissick Museum, University of South Carolina, 1998.

Quimby, Ian M. G., and Scott T. Swank, eds. *Perspectives on American Folk Art*. New York: W. W. Norton, 1980. A Winterthur Book.

Revivalism and Eclecticism: The Mid- and Late Nineteenth Century

Ames, Kenneth L. *Death in the Dining Room and Other Tales of Victorian Culture*. Philadelphia: Temple University Press, 1992.

Burke, Doreen Bolger, et al. *In Pursuit of Beauty: Americans and the Aesthetic Movement*. New York: Rizzoli in association with the Metropolitan Museum of Art, 1986.

Brooklyn Museum. *The American Renaissance, 1876–1917*. New York: Brooklyn Museum, 1979. Distributed by Pantheon Books, New York.

Howe, Katherine S., and David B. Warren. *The Gothic Revival Style in America, 1830–1870*. Houston: Museum of Fine Arts, 1976.

Howe, Katherine S., et al. *Herter Brothers: Furniture and Interiors for a Gilded Age*. New York: Harry N. Abrams in association with the Museum of Fine Arts, Houston, 1994.

Venable, Charles. *Silver in America, 1840–1940: A Century of Splendor*. Dallas: Dallas Museum of Art, 1994. Distributed by Harry N. Abrams, New York.

Voorsanger, Catherine Hoover, and John K. Howat, eds. *Art and the Empire City: New York, 1825–1861*. New York: Metropolitan Museum of Art, 2000.

Reaction and Reform: The Late Nineteenth and Early Twentieth Centuries

Boris, Eileen. *Art and Labor: Ruskin, Morris, and the Craftsman Ideal in America*. Philadelphia: Temple University Press, 1986.

Kaplan, Wendy, et al. *The Art That Is Life: The Arts and Crafts Movement in America, 1875–1920*. Boston: Bulfinch Press in association with the Museum of Fine Arts, 1987.

Kardon, Janet, ed. *The Ideal Home: The History of Twentieth-Century American Craft, 1900–1920*. New York: Harry N. Abrams in association with the American Craft Museum, 1993.

Meyer, Merrilee Boyd, ed. *Inspiring Reform: Boston's Arts and Crafts Movement*. Wellesley, MA: Davis Museum and Cultural Center, Wellesley College, 1997. Distributed by Harry N. Abrams, New York.

Modernism and Design: The Early and Mid-Twentieth Century

Benton, Tim, Charlotte Benton, and Ghislaine Wood. *Art Deco, 1910–1939*. London: V & A Publications, 2003.

Davies, Karen. *At Home in Manhattan: Modern Decorative Arts, 1925 to the Depression*. New Haven, CT: Yale University Art Gallery, 1983.

Eidelberg, Martin P., ed. *Design 1935–1965: What Modern Was; Selections from the Liliane and David M. Stewart Collection, Le Musée des arts décoratifs de Montréal*. Montréal: Musée des arts décoratifs de Montréal; New York: Harry N. Abrams, 1991.

Hiesinger, Kathryn B., and George H. Marcus. *Landmarks of Twentieth-Century Design: An Illustrated Handbook*. New York: Abbeville Press, 1993.

Kirkham, Pat, ed. *Women Designers in the U.S.A., 1900–2000: Diversity and Difference*. New Haven, CT: Yale University Press, 2002.

Stern, Jewel. *Modernism in American Silver: Twentieth Century Design*. New Haven, CT: Yale University Press, 2005.

Venable, Charles L., et al. *China and Glass in America, 1880–1980: From Tabletop to TV Tray*. Dallas: Dallas Museum of Art, 2000. Distributed by Harry N. Abrams, New York.

Wilson, Richard Guy, Dianne H. Pilgrim, and Dickran Tashjian. *The Machine Age in America, 1918–1941*. New York: Brooklyn Museum in association with Harry N. Abrams, 1986.

The Studio Craft Movement in America: The Late Twentieth Century

Clark, Garth. *American Ceramics: 1876 to the Present*. Rev. ed. New York: Abbeville Press, 1987.

Cooke, Edward S., Jr. *New American Furniture: The Second Generation of Studio Furnituremakers*. Boston: Museum of Fine Arts, 1989.

Cooke, Edward S., Jr., Gerald W. R. Ward, and Kelly H. L'Ecuyer. *The Maker's Hand: American Studio Furniture, 1940–1990*. Boston: MFA Publications, 2003.

Drutt, Helen W., and Peter Dormer. *Jewelry of Our Time: Art, Ornament, and Obsession*. New York: Rizzoli, 1995.

Fairbanks, Jonathan L., and Kenworth W. Moffett. *Directions in Contemporary American Ceramics*. Boston: Museum of Fine Arts, 1984.

Fairbanks, Jonathan L., Pat Warner, et al. *Glass Today by American Studio Artists*. Boston: Museum of Fine Arts, 1997.

Lauria, Jo, et al. *Color and Fire: Defining Moments in Studio Ceramics, 1950–2000*. Los Angeles: Los Angeles County Museum of Art in association with Rizzoli, 2000.

Layton, Peter. *Glass Art*. London: A&C Black; Seattle: University of Washington Press, 1996.

Nordness, Lee. *Objects: USA*. New York: Viking Press, 1970.

Taragin, Davira Spiro. *Contemporary Crafts and the Saxe Collection*. New York: Hudson Hills Press; Toledo: Toledo Museum of Art, 1993. Distributed by National Book Network, Lanham, MD.

Figure Illustrations

p. 11, fig. 1
Pitcher
Tiffany and Company (1837–present)
New York, New York, 1875
Silver, copper
H. 20.5 cm , w. 10.6 cm, d. 9.5 cm, wt. 276.4
gm (H. 8¼ in., w. 4³⁄₁₆ in., d. 3¾ in., wt. 8 oz.
17 dwt. 18 gr.)
Gift of Gideon F. T. Reed 77.61

p. 10, fig. 2
View of Boston Common (embroidered
picture)
Hannah Otis (1732–1801)
Boston, Massachusetts, about 1750
Wool, silk, metallic threads, and beads on
linen ground; predominantey tent stitch;
original frame and glass
61.6 x 134 cm (24¼ x 52¾ in.)
Gift of a Friend of the Department of
American Decorative Arts and Sculpture, a
Supporter of the Department of American
Decorative Arts and Sculpture, Barbara L.
and Theodore B. Alfond, and Samuel A.
Otis; and William Francis Warden Fund,
Harriet Otis Cruft Fund, Otis Norcross
Fund, Susan Cornelia Warren Fund, Arthur
Tracy Cabot Fund, Seth K. Sweetser Fund,
Edwin E. Jack Fund, Helen B. Sweeney
Fund, William E. Nickerson Fund, Arthur
Mason Knapp Fund, Samuel Putnam Avery
Fund, Benjamin Pierce Cheney Fund, and
Mary L. Smith Fund 1996.26

p. 12, fig. 3
Appeal to the Great Spirit
Cyrus E. Dallin (1861–1944)
Designed in Arlington or Boston,
Massachusetts, cast in Paris, 1909
Bronze, green patina, lost wax cast
H. 309.9 cm, w. 111.1 cm, d. 260.4 cm (H.
122 in., w. 43¾ in., d. 102½ in.)
Gift of Peter C. Brooks and others 13.380

p. 14, fig. 4
Bureau dressing table
Edmund Townsend (1736–1811)
Newport, Rhode Island, 1765–85
San Domingo mahogany, Cuban mahogany,
whitewood, chestnut
H. 85.4 cm, w. 87.6 cm, d. 47.9 cm (H. 33⅝
in., w. 34½ in., d. 18⅞ in.)
The M. and M. Karolik Collection of
Eighteenth-Century American Arts 41.579

p. 15, fig. 5
Porringer
Thomas Knox Emery (1781–1815)
Boston, Massachusetts, about 1805–15
Silver
H. 5.2 cm, w. 21 cm, diam. rim 14 cm, wt.
270 gm (H. 2⅛ in., w. 8¼ in., diam. rim 5½
in., wt. 8 oz. 13 dwt. 14 gr.)
Bequest of Charles Hitchcock Tyler 32.385

p. 17, fig. 6
Pair of tulip-celery vases
Boston and Sandwich Glass Company
(1826–1888)
Sandwich, Massachusetts, 1845–65
Pressed glass
Left: H. 24.8 cm (9¾ in.)
Right: H. 26 cm (10¼ in.)
Gift of Dorothy-Lee Jones 1994.207–208

p. 18, fig. 7 (from left to right)
Wine cup
Peter Young (active 1775–95)
New York or Albany, New York, 1775–95
Pewter
H. 21.6 cm (8½ in.)
Bequest of Mrs. Stephen S. Fitz-Gerald
64.1743

p. 18, **Flagon**
Samuel Danforth (1772–1827)
Hartford, Connecticut, 1795–1816
Pewter
H. 29.2 cm (11½ in.)
Bequest of Mrs. Stephen S. Fitz-Gerald
64.1733

p. 18, **Teapot**
Thomas Danforth Boardman (1784–1873)
Hartford, Connecticut, about 1804–60
Pewter
H. 22.2 cm (8¾ in.)
Bequest of Mrs. Stephen S. Fitz-Gerald
64.1794

p. 19, fig. 8
Map of the World
Abbey Perkins (active about 1811)
Chelsea (now Norwich), Connecticut, 1811
Pen, ink, and watercolor on paper
45.4 x 68.9 cm (17⅞ x 27⅛ in.)
Bequest of Maxim Karolik for the M. and
M. Karolik Collection of American
Watercolors and Drawings, 1800–1875
1995.768

p. 25, fig. 9

Headstone for John Foster

Attributed to the Charlestown Stonecutter

Probably Charlestown, Massachusetts, 1681

Slate

H. 125.7 cm, w. 58.4 cm, d. 6 cm (H. 49½ in., w. 23 in., d. 2⅜ in.)

Museum of Fine Arts, Boston; lent by the Boston Parks and Recreation Commission from the Dorchester Burial Ground

p. 27, fig. 10

Attributed to Thomas Smith (about 1650–1691)

Major Thomas Savage

Boston, Massachusetts, 1679

Oil on canvas mounted on Masonite

106.7 x 94 cm (42 x 37 in.)

Museum of Fine Arts, Boston, Bequest of Henry Lee Shattuck in memory of the late Morris Gray   1983.35

p. 55, fig. 11

John Greenwood (1727–1792)

The Greenwood-Lee Family

Boston, Massachusetts, about 1747

Oil on canvas

141 x 175.6 cm (55½ x 69⅛ in.)

Museum of Fine Arts, Boston, Bequest of Henry Lee Shattuck in memory of the late Morris Gray   1983.34

p. 57, fig. 12

Tapestry cover

Peru, about 1600–700 or later

Cotton and wool interlocked and dovetailed tapestry

238.5 x 216 cm (93⅞ x 85⅛ in.)

Museum of Fine Arts, Boston, Charles Potter King Fund   67.25

p. 65, fig. 13

John Greenwood (1727–1792)

Mrs. Henry Bromfield (Margaret Fayerweather)

Boston, Massachusetts, about 1749

Oil on canvas

92.4 x 65.7 cm (36⅜ x 25⅞ in.)

Museum of Fine Arts, Boston, Emily L. Ainsley Fund   62.173

p. 77, fig. 14

Side chair

Thomas Hooper (active about 1750)

England, about 1750–60

Mahogany, beech

H. 94.6 cm, w. 59.1 cm, d. 48.9 cm (H. 37¼ in., w. 23¼ in., d. 19¼ in.)

Museum of Fine Arts, Boston, Gift of Mrs. Joshua Crane Sr. in memory of her husband   30.726

p. 77, fig. 15

"Chairs" (detail).

From Thomas Chippendale, *The Gentleman and Cabinet-Maker's Director: Being a Large Collection of the Most Elegant and Useful Designs of Household Furniture, in the Most Fashionable Taste*, 3rd ed. (London: published by the author, 1762), plate 14

Museum of Fine Arts, Boston, Gift of Maxim Karolik   31.995

p. 79, fig. 16

John Singleton Copley (1738–1815)

Paul Revere

Boston, Massachusetts, 1768

Oil on canvas

89.2 x 72.4 cm (35⅛ x 28½ in.)

Museum of Fine Arts, Boston, Gift of Joseph W. Revere, William B. Revere and Edward H. R. Revere   30.781

p. 89, fig. 17

Parlor from Oak Hill, South Danvers, Massachusetts, about 1800–1801, as installed at the Museum of Fine Arts, Boston; design and carving attributed to Samuel McIntire (1757–1811). Photograph © Lou Jones 1999.

p. 90, fig. 18

Henry Sargent (1770–1845)

The Dinner Party

Boston, Massachusetts, about 1821

Oil on canvas

156.5 x 126.4 cm (61⅝ x 49¾ in.)

Museum of Fine Arts, Boston, Gift of Mrs. Horatio Appleton Lamb in memory of Mr. and Mrs. Winthrop Sargent   19.13

p. 91, fig. 19

Henry Sargent (1770–1845)

The Tea Party

Boston, Massachusetts, 1824

Oil on canvas

171.1 x 133 cm (64⅜ x 52⅜ in.)

Museum of Fine Arts, Boston, Gift of Mrs. Horatio Appleton Lamb in memory of Mr. and Mrs. Winthrop Sargent   19.12

p. 93, fig. 20

Pitcher

William Ellis Tucker Factory Porcelain Company (active 1826–1838)

Philadelphia, Pennsylvania, about 1830

Porcelain with underglaze decoration and gilding over the glaze

H. 22.9 cm, w. 20.3 cm, d. 15.2 cm (H. 9½ in., w. 8 in., d. 6 in.)

Museum of Fine Arts, Boston, Gift of Miss Aimée and Miss Rosamond Lamb in memory of their mother Mrs. Horatio Appleton Lamb   56.1246

p. 105, fig. 21

United States quarter dollar (obverse and reverse)

Designed by John Reich (1768–1833); engraved by Reich and Robert Scot (died 1823); minted at Philadelphia, Pennsylvania

Philadelphia, Pennsylvania, 1818

Silver

Diam. 2.7 cm (1¹⁄₁₆ in.)

Museum of Fine Arts, Boston, The Sidney A. and Ellen M. Wien Collection—Given in their memory by Claire W. and Richard P. Morse   2004.808

p. 117, fig. 22

Plate

Attributed to John Neis (1785–1867)

Upper Salford Township, Montgomery County, Pennsylvania, 1834

Redware with slip and sgraffito decoration

Diam. 27.3 cm (10¾ in.)

Museum of Fine Arts, Boston, Anonymous gift   02.323

p. 118, fig. 23

Mariner's compass bed quilt

New England, 1840–50

Cotton plain weave, printed, pieced and quilted, plain weave backing

232 x 231 cm (91⁵⁄₁₆ x 90¹⁵⁄₁₆ in.)

Museum of Fine Arts, Boston, Gift of Mrs. George C. Seybolt   1999.248

p. 132, fig. 24

Souvenir kerchief from Philadelphia Centennial Exhibition

Probably Philadelphia, Pennsylvania, about 1876

Printed cotton

66.2 x 66.8 cm (26¹⁄₁₆ x 26⁵⁄₁₆ in.)

Museum of Fine Arts, Boston, Bequest of Maxim Karolik   64.687

p. 134, fig. 25

Enrico Meneghelli (1853–after 1912)

The Picture Gallery at the Old Museum

Boston, Massachusetts, 1879

Oil on paperboard

40.6 x 30.5 cm (16 x 12 in.)

Museum of Fine Arts, Boston, Gift of Hollis French   RES.12.2

p. 157, fig. 26

Sara Galner decorates the wares at the Paul Revere Pottery, about 1915. Photograph courtesy of Dr. David L. Bloom and family.

p. 159, fig. 27

Tall-back side chair

Made by John W. Ayers & Co. (1890–1913)

Designed by Frank Lloyd Wright (1867–1959) for the Warren Hickox House, Kankakee, Illinois

Chicago, Illinois, about 1900

Oak, leather

H. 180.3 cm, w. 47 cm, d. 48.9 cm (H. 71 in., w. 18½ in., d. 19¼ in.)

Courtesy of American Decorative Art 1900 Foundation

p. 167, fig. 28

Studio of Arthur Stone, Gardner, Massachusetts, about 1908. Arthur J. Stone Papers, Museum of Fine Arts, Boston, Gift of Alma Bent.

p. 179, fig. 29

Length of furnishing fabric

Du Pont Rayon Company, design attributed to Thomas Lamb (1896–1988)

New York, New York, about 1930

Printed rayon plain weave

274.3 x 89 cm (108 x 35 in.)

Museum of Fine Arts, Boston, Museum purchase with funds donated by the Textile and Costume Society, Museum of Fine Arts, Boston   2003.309

p. 181, fig. 30

Joseph Stella (1877–1946)

Old Brooklyn Bridge

New York, New York, about 1940

Oil on canvas

193.7 x 173.4 cm (76¼ x 68¼ in.)

Museum of Fine Arts, Boston, Gift of Susan Morse Hilles in memory of Paul Hellmuth   1980.197

p. 195, fig. 31

Wirework brooch

Margret Craver (born 1907)

New York, New York, about 1945

Gold wire

4.8 x 1.9 cm (1⅞ x ¾ in.)

Museum of Fine Arts, Boston, Gift of Margret Craver Withers   1993.834

p. 197, fig. 32

Settee

Wendell Castle (born 1932)

Rochester, New York, 1979

Cherry

H. 91.4 cm, w. 147.3 cm, d. 61 cm (H. 36 in., w. 58 in., d. 24 in.)

Museum of Fine Arts, Boston, Museum purchase with funds donated by the National Endowment for the Arts and the Deborah M. Noonan Foundation   1979.266

p. 206, fig. 33

Chest

Charles James Prendergast (1863–1948)

New York, New York, and Westport,
Connecticut, 1926–27

Pine and gessoed wood, carved, painted,
and gilded

H. 50.8 cm, w. 132.1 cm, d. 49.5 cm (H. 20
in., w. 52 in., d. 19½ in.)

Museum of Fine Arts, Boston, Purchased
through John H. and Ernestine A. Payne
Fund   67.732

p. 210

Spectral-Luma Ellipse 2000

Tom Patti (born 1943)

Pittsfield, Massachusetts, 2000

Glass, synthetic materials

294.6 x 602 cm (116 x 237 in.)

Museum of Fine Arts, Boston, Museum
purchase with funds donated by the
Ladies Committee Associates as a
Millennium Gift   2000.686.1–7

Index

Page numbers in italics indicate illustration captions.